Some Pretty Impressive Results: Final Reports from Our Original Project Managers

I didn't know how effective The Husband Project would be until we tried it out on some real-live marriages. Judging from the project managers' comments below, good things are in store for you and your guy.

"Wow! I can't think of anything more powerful a woman can do for her marriage than *The Husband Project.* There will be thousands of smiling men as a result of this great book. I highly recommend it for every woman. Shhh! It's a secret, but I've already started on *The Husband Project* to bless my man!"—Pam Farrel, author of *Men Are Like Waffles, Women Are Like Spaghetti* and *Red-Hot Monogamy*

"I couldn't put the book down. With great insight into the heart, desires, and needs of men, Kathi Lipp has put together a 'can't miss' guide to a better marriage. It has wit (I'm still laughing at the "Worship Macarena") and wisdom. My favorite projects are 2, 14, and 20—oh, and all the bonus projects (hey, I'm a guy)."—Steve Jordahl, producer, Family News in Focus, Focus on the Family

"Have a sizzling affair—with your spouse! *The Husband Project* brims with the kind of secret and surprising advice that'll help you become the wife he desires. A fun, innovative, and practical book."—Mary E. DeMuth, wife of one, mother of three, author of *Ordinary Mom, Extraordinary God* and *Authentic Parenting in a Postmodern Culture*

"Although camouflaged as an adorably written and delightfully funny book, in reality *The Husband Project* is a powerful tool to facilitate a more solid and fulfilling marriage. Chock-full of fresh ideas and practical insights, this book is inspiring and entertaining—and the 21-day plan is easy to follow. It's sure to infuse your marriage with renewed passion and reawakened love."—Paula Friedrichsen, speaker and author of *The Man You Always Wanted Is the One You Already Have*

"If your romance has turned into a nightly sitcom, Kathi Lipp has some fun ways to put the courtship back into your marriage, not to mention bonding time with your girlfriends. An excellent resource for all things relationship and getting the most out of a joyous journey alongside your husband."—Kristin Billerbeck, author of *What a Girl Wants* and *The Trophy Wives Club*

The Husband Project

Kathi Lipp

HARVEST HOUSE PUBLISHERS
EUGENE, OREGON

Cover design by Left Coast Design, Portland, OR

Cover illustration © Krieg Barrie

Backcover author photo by Jessi Enguerra

Published in association with the literary agency of WordServe Literary Group, Ltd., 10152 S. Knoll Circle, Highlands Ranch, CO 80130

THE HUSBAND PROJECT
Copyright © 2009 by Kathi Lipp
Published by Harvest House Publishers
Eugene, Oregon 97402
www.harvesthousepublishers.com

Library of Congress Cataloging-in-Publication Data
Lipp, Kathi, 1967-
The husband project / Kathi Lipp.
p. cm.
Includes bibliographical references.
ISBN 978-0-7369-2522-8 (pbk.)
1. Marriage—Religious aspects—Christianity. 2. Wives—Religious life. I. Title.
BV4596.M3L57 2009
248.8'435—dc22

2008020671

Printed in the United States of America

09 10 11 12 13 14 15 16 / BP-SK / 11 10 9 8 7 6 5 4

This book is completely and totally dedicated to my husband, Roger Lipp. If it had not been for the questionable judgment you showed when you said, "I think you need to give this speaking and writing thing to God and see what He does with it," none of this would have ever happened.

I still go throughout my day, stop, and pretty much cannot believe that I get to be married to you.

Acknowledgments

To my son, Justen Hunter, and my daughter, Kimber Hunter, for letting me practice being a mom on you and for sharing my love of written words so much that you gave me untold amounts of grace while writing this book. Not only are you both gifted writers, you are turning out to be great people.

To my stepkids, Amanda and Jeremy, for sharing your amazing dad and your beautiful lives with me. It is an honor to be your stepmom.

To my parents, Bill and Connie Richerson, for your unwavering support of any crazy thing I wanted to do, and the love to see me through.

To Roger's parents, Pastor Dean and Betty Dobson, and Dewayne and Mary Jane Lipp, who have raised an incredible man and shown him firsthand what true love looks like.

To Angela Bowen, my friend and prayer girl, accountability partner and believer of all good things. You have to know that none of this would have happened without you.

To Kim and Doug Gonsalves and Chris and Vikki Francis, I pray that the generosity you have shown me will pour over into others' lives. You four are walking miracles and tangible examples of Christ's love.

To Pastor Steve and Shannon Jordahl and Pastor Jim and Kim Meyer. You have left a spiritual legacy that you'll never fully recognize until Jesus tells you Himself. Thank you for letting me be a part of it.

To the amazing force of nature that is my agent, Rachelle Gardner, and to Rod Morris of Harvest House. Thank you for having the time to listen to my crazy little idea about a husband book and for having a passion to see marriages helped and healed. It is an honor to work with you both.

To my critique group, Cathy Armstrong, Judy Squire, Pat Sikora, Kathie Williams, and most of all Katie Vorreiter. You have helped me find my voice, and at the same time made me think I might be able to someday use it to write a book.

To the other amazing writers who have loved and supported me along the way, including Lynn Walker, Susy Flory, and Cheri Gregory.

To my prayer partners, and Advisory Board, including Carol Alexander, Terri Gohner, Marci Maples, Sherry Eager, Sheri Wideman, Penny Sands, Lynette Furstenberg, Kelli Simmerok, Pam Kelley, Cindy Anderson, Mary Dickerson, Dana Galasso, Patti Johnston, Michelle Smith. Each and every one of you is precious to me.

To our brothers and their others: Brian, Lucinda, Randy, Debbie, Rick, and Linda. We are blessed to be surrounded by such love.

To Pastor Scott Simmerok and the people of Church on the Hill in San Jose, CA. Thank you for being His hands and feet to our family.

Finally, to Teresa Drake. God's timing is a crazy thing, and I am amazed at the talent, encouragement, and incredible gift that He lent me through you at just the right time. God has amazing things in store for you. Glad I got to be there to see the seeds sprout.

Contents

Week Two Projects

Week Three Projects

Tools of The Husband Project

Laying a Foundation

Preparing for The Husband Project

1

Why The Husband Project?

"Kathi, a couple of us need to quit the project."

I couldn't believe what Angela was saying. Quit The Husband Project? We'd just started that weekend.

"Ange, are you kidding me? Why do you want to quit already?"

"I was talking to some of the other girls, and because we're being so nice, our husbands are becoming suspicious. They think we're all having affairs!"

Apparently, there's a bigger need for The Husband Project than even I could have expected.

The Beginning of The Husband Project

At my busy church in San Jose, California, I serve in a variety of roles. Some of the roles I have played have been on the programming team with my husband, Roger (who is the director of the Worship Arts Ministry), leading Bible studies and small groups and taking meals to people who are sick or having babies. But my favorite role by far is mentoring women.

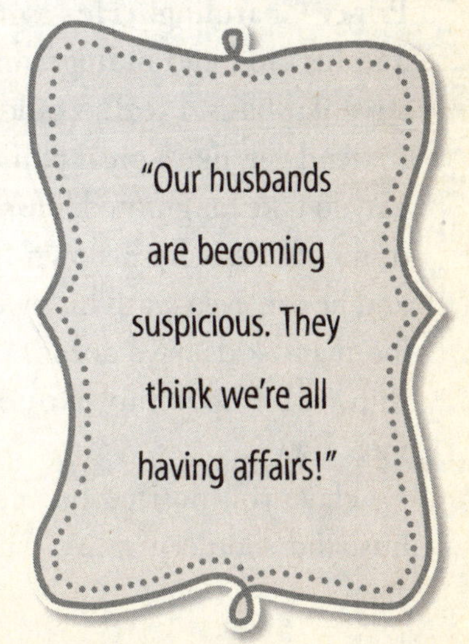

The girls I mentor are smart, funny, and committed to serving God. They really are amazing. However, like most wives I know, they have a tendency to "share" about their husbands.

"He's never home. I feel like I'm single—but with an extra person to clean up after."

"Why is it when he's watching our kids it's *babysitting?*"

"We used to be romantic, but now our idea of romance is reading take-out menus together."

The "sharing" started to concern me. I wasn't judging these girls, trust me. I found myself slipping every once in a while, saying something "endearing" about my husband while rolling my eyes.

A Change in Perspective

I know the importance of loving and honoring my husband, and like every other lesson in my life, I learned it the hard way. (Why can't I ever learn things while eating chocolates and shopping?)

I married in my early twenties, and two babies came along shortly after the marriage vows. In retrospect, I can see that as soon as I discovered the wonders of a Diaper Genie, my concentration shifted from my husband to the day-to-day care of my kids. With a full-time job thrown in, the goal of making my husband feel special dropped way down on my priority list.

After a painful marriage and divorce, I am now remarried to an amazing guy. When new friends meet him they say, "Oh, so this is Prince Charming!" He's a great father and stepdad, and he loves me and his God and indulges my passion for fat-free coconut yogurt on a regular basis. I really couldn't ask for a better guy.

And yet, like a great pair of comfortable flip-flops, he's sometimes easy to take for granted. He's always there—not demanding anything of me. He can fix his own frozen pizza when I'm too busy to cook, and he can even wash his own socks in a pinch. When work deadlines loom and kids have dozens of activities, I sometimes let my relationship with Rog fall to sixth or seventh on my "Hey, pay attention to me!" list.

Have you noticed our culture has a one-way expectation that a husband should give his wife what she "needs" (sending flowers to work, doing his share of the dirty work around the house, being a great dad, remembering and celebrating anniversaries) without asking for anything in return? But, as we know, this fantasy man isn't a real husband; he's a character in a dime-store romance novel.

The kind of marriage I want is one in which we're both doing all we can to honor and love each other, putting each other's needs above our own. Philippians 2:3-4 says it best: "Do nothing out of selfish ambition or vain conceit, but in humility consider others better than yourselves. Each of you should look not only to your own interests, but also to the interests of others."

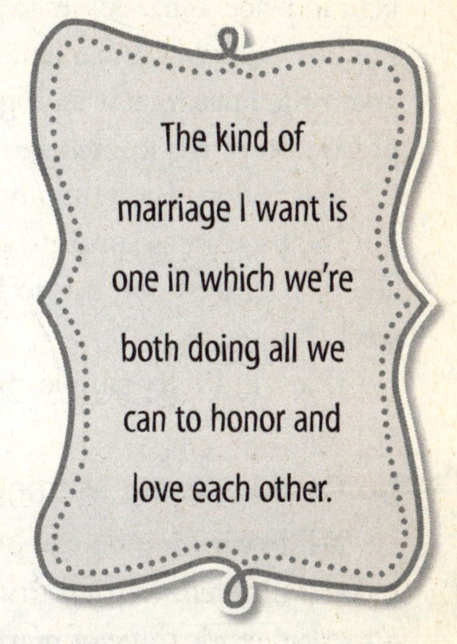

I want this for both of us. The reality is, however, I have control only over my own actions.

Enter The Husband Project

I tried different ideas with some of my friends at church—a variety of "husband encouragement programs." Most seemed like a lot of work and not much fun. You see, I have the attention span of a third-grader who's just spent six straight hours on Xbox. So I needed something short, doable, and exciting. We, as stressed-out and overworked wives and moms, don't need to feel burdened by another item on our to-do lists.

So I started thinking and praying about what would truly make my husband feel loved...and maybe even feel lucky to be married to me. I made up a list and began practicing on Roger. Some of the ideas (buying him a gift card to his favorite restaurant and surprising him with an impromptu date) were big hits. Others (like opening mystery clues for an all-day adventure) were, let's say, less than successful.

After several flops (hey, I thought the guys at his work would think that his lunch sack covered in hearts was adorable) I finally got desperate. I asked him, "Okay, what would make you feel loved?" And yes, I felt pretty pathetic to be asking. After showing him the list, he gave me thumbs up or down on several of the items. I now had a much clearer plan in place. No, cookies in the shapes of bunnies were not necessary. Homemade raw cookie dough, however, was a big thumbs-up. Yes, I asked the questions. I have gone where women fear to tread. I am in possession of the knowledge of what men (or at least my man) like.

This is how The Husband Project was born.

The premise is simple: You and two other friends (your accountability partners) commit to bless your husbands every day for three weeks, in secret.

That's it. Pretty simple, granted. But not always easy.

No Cookie-Cutter Marriages

While working on the projects, I talked with friends of all ages, in very different marital situations. Some of my friends were in the oh-so-romantic stage of marriage. You're just done in by how beautifully he shaves. As you pick up his clothes from the bedroom floor, you just can't help but giggle at how adorable it is that he never puts anything away.

On the other side of the spectrum, I have girlfriends who cannot stand to be in the same room with their husbands while they're breathing. The "inhale-exhale" is enough to make them want to take up residence at a nice studio apartment in town.

And then there are the other 94 percent of us.

We're the ones who love our husbands but have fallen into a comfortable routine (*comfortable* often meaning, *you don't bug me and I won't bug you*). We're partners in parenting and contributors to financial matters. We've negotiated the household chores ("I'll do the dishes if you keep the car from making funny noises") and keep each other on schedule for the dentist and the occasional oil change.

We like our husbands, for the most part. And they like us, for the most part. While this is okay, it's definitely not what we were anticipating as we planned our weddings and dreamed about our happily-ever-after lives.

I have to admit, I'm writing this book for me and my friends—the 94 percent who want better relationships with our men and are willing to be creative, thoughtful, and possibly daring enough to break out some lingerie to get it.

"But He Doesn't Even Notice"

Some women who have tried the projects for a few days wondered if it's even worth it. After doing several of the projects, they complained that their husbands have barely noticed.

So, if you're wearing your cute jeans to meet your husband in the evenings, leaving bags of Gummi Bears for him in his car, and wearing skimpier and skimpier lingerie to bed each night without comment from your man, don't be discouraged.

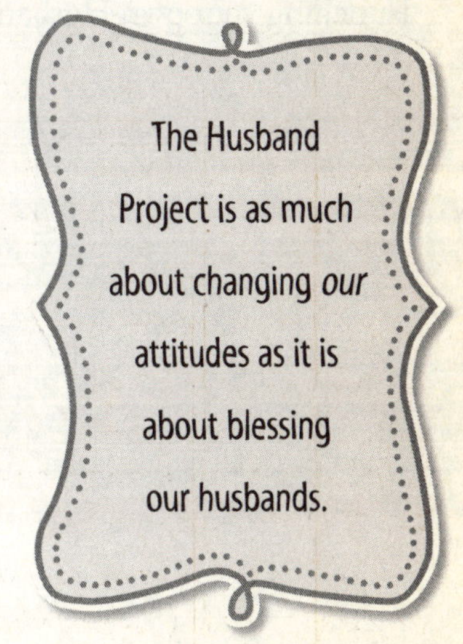

Working on The Husband Project is a lot like working on your prayer life. I recently committed to set aside a chunk of time daily to pray. As I devote more time to prayer and meditation, I'm realizing that my requests are less about asking God to make things go my way and more about asking God to change my heart to follow Him and *His* plans for me.

The Husband Project is as much about changing *our* attitudes as it is about blessing our husbands. It's great to get positive reinforcement, and when you do, write it down so you can remember it and tailor the way that you show your love in the future. But even when your husband says nothing, you have the knowledge that you have actively shown him love and support. That's the true gift of The Husband Project.

If you still need some affirmation (and who doesn't?) look for it in other healthy places. In my case I have a friend, Lynn, who sends me a small gift whenever I complete a writing goal. Even if I don't sell an article, I still have the hope of some great Snoopy stickers in the mail.

Ask your accountability partners to celebrate your successes with you. Perhaps if each of you does your daily project for seven days, you give each other a $5 Starbucks card, or if you do all 21 days, you spend an afternoon together at the spa. Be creative. As it says in Hebrews 10:24, "And let us consider how we may spur one another on toward love and good deeds." A grande latte could be an excellent way to start.

In the next chapter, I'll walk you through a step-by-step guide for launching your own Husband Project.

2

A Quick How-to Guide for The Husband Project

The purpose of The Husband Project is to spend 21 days loving and supporting your husband, intentionally. Remember, this is a secret. Hide the book at work, in your car, anywhere that your husband will not see it.

Here's your step-by step guide to doing The Project.

1. Read through all of the projects.

This is your chance to get a feel for all 21 of the projects. Be sure to use all of this book. Make notes in the margins, scribble and doodle on the pages, and start to think about ways to tailor each project to your husband.

2. Find two other friends who want to do The Husband Project and will hold you accountable.

It doesn't matter if they're phone friends, Internet buddies, or face-to-face girlfriends you meet with at Starbucks down the street. Location is not important; consistency is. Figure out a time to spend together (after everyone has read through the book) to come up with a plan for when and how you're going to do the projects.

3. Sign The Husband Project Accountability Covenant (see page 33).

4. Decide on a start date.

It can be tomorrow or two weeks from now. Mark it in a big bold way on your kitchen calendar. Set up reminders on your computer. I recommend that you give yourself a couple of days to get ramped up and pull together a plan that you're excited about—one you know will bless your guy.

5. Look over the projects and come up with your personalized plans.

You decide how you're going to bless your husband each day. I've provided a variety of ideas, but it's up to you to decide how you'll carry out each day's project. Get creative and come up with a new and wonderful way to raise your husband's eyebrows.

Write down in advance what you're going to do for each day in the space provided at the end of each project. Then copy the plan for that day on The Husband Project Planner at the back of this book.

I have recently lost a bunch of weight. One of the key elements in making this happen (besides putting down the chocolate) has been to write down what I'm going to eat rather than keeping a log of what I already ate. Put purpose and a plan to work. That's how you'll experience winning results.

As you read through the projects, you will start to notice a theme developing. Lots of the projects are centered around certain topics: food, encouragement, your appearance, and acts of service. I promise this is not a case of me just running out of ideas. These were the types of projects that the women who did The Husband Project got the best results with.

Do your best to complete each project each day and see if you don't agree that these projects are some of the ones that will bless your husband the most.

You'll also need to make some specific plans along the way. Is there a night when you'll need babysitting? Get on the phone now. Is there a special candy that you can get only online and need to order now for next Saturday's project? Order it in advance so you'll be ready.

6. Share your project plans with your accountability partners.

I recommend that you make copies of your planner pages to share with your accountability partners. (There's a Project Planner in the Tools of The Husband Project section at the back of this book.) That way, you can commit to pray for each other as well as lend support on days that may be particularly challenging. Who knows, your accountability partners may have some great, creative ideas to share.

7. Be flexible.

If one of the projects doesn't line up with your husband's schedule, swap it for another day. If food does nothing for him, find another way to treat your hubby. This is all about connecting with him. The intention of The Husband Project is not to make you crazy, but to find new ways to bless and support your husband. Just do *something*, intentionally, every day.

3

Why 21 Days?

"Jill, I have to be honest with you. I hate this—and by extension, I am growing to hate you. I hope you realize it's nothing personal."

Jill understood, but she was not going to grant me the "Get Out of Exercising" card I was looking for.

"Kath—just give it three weeks. I promise you, it won't feel like you're walking to the guillotine every day if you just stick with it."

When I was in my early twenties, I had the opportunity to do some short-term missions work in Japan. While some of my friends were toiling on the plains of Africa, digging wells and starting community businesses in remote villages, I decided on a less *Survivor*-esque adventure by teaching conversational English in air-conditioned classrooms near Kyoto. (Hey, we all have our own level of roughing it. Mine was living two trains away from a McDonald's.)

After the first week, I realized I had a big problem. While in the United States, I relied on my bright orange '74 Honda to get me the two and a half blocks to the grocery store. Walking was for losers who didn't have cars. However, in Japan, my main form of transportation was pedal power. I had a pink bike (bell and flowered basket included) that I rode everywhere. The problem was that after a few blocks, I was not only winded, I was completely wiped. That, plus the fact that I lived on the fourth floor of my apartment building with no elevator, showed me all too clearly which of my muscles hadn't been used in a while. I knew that I needed to get into better physical condition if I was going to survive the year abroad.

One of my expatriate coworkers, Jill, was the undisputed aerobics queen of Kyoto. She was also one of those annoying people who just could not imagine starting her day without some carrot-wheatgrass juice and a "quick" 45-minute workout.

No one liked her.

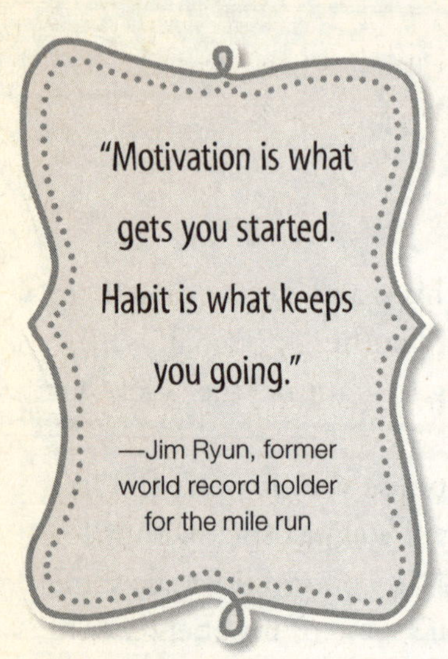

OK, perhaps I am projecting a bit. There were plenty of people who loved Jill. I just wasn't one of them as she waxed poetic about the number of calories burned by abdominal crunches.

After foolishly opening up to her about my struggle with getting around town, "Jumping-Jacks Jill" promised me she could whip me into shape in no time at all.

Jill showed up at my apartment every day with a Jane Fonda workout video and a smile. After the first couple of workouts, I desperately wanted out. I spent the next couple of weeks trying to come up with every excuse I could muster to get out of our healthy bonding time.

"I'm tired."

"I'm having my period."

"I'm concerned that my downstairs neighbors are experiencing aftershocks."

"I don't know how that hammer got jammed in the VCR."

It didn't matter; Jill was consistent. She already had the habit of daily exercise built into her life. Now she was trying to indoctrinate me into her sick little plan.

By the beginning of the third week, I had moved from outright hostility to begrudging resignation. I wasn't exactly excited to see Jill on my doorstep each morning, but I figured it was easier to just get the exercise out of the way than to keep breaking the VCR.

Now, here's the weird thing…

After about a month, Jill had to go to Tokyo for some work-related training. I thought, *Oh, thank God. I need a day off from all of this! I* *can sleep in, I can read a book. I don't have to jump around like a fool...*I looked forward to my day off as though it were a Macy's preseason sale.

When that glorious Tuesday arrived, I woke up and felt odd and disoriented. I was kind of lost, just puttering around my apartment, not knowing what to do with myself, completely out of sorts. And then it hit me.

I missed exercising.

I couldn't believe it either. Jill had sucked me over to the Dark Side. After just a few weeks, the habit of exercise had become so ingrained in me that not only did I no longer consider it a burden, I actually missed it.

You may start off the whole Husband Project champing at the bit. "My husband's not going to know what hit him! I'm going to blow him away with all the love and affection he can handle. Gourmet dinners, creative and meaningful Bonus Projects, and all the praise I can think of."

Then you get to Project 3—and you're tired of all this already.

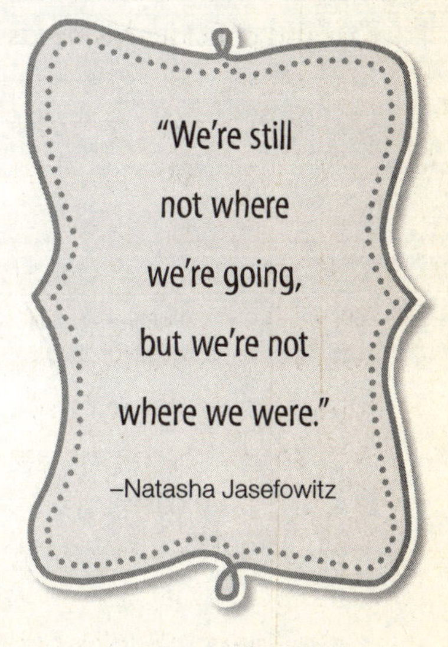

"I don't have time to do all this nice stuff. Don't you know I have a life outside of my marriage?"

"I'm tired."

"I'm having my period."

"We don't have the money."

"Once he starts acting nice, I'll start acting nice."

That's why it's so important to commit to the 21 days, right up front.

I was told over and over by an über-exuberant gym teacher that it takes 21 days to build or thoroughly break a habit. I believe that building good habits to encourage our husbands means putting our relationship on "project status." After the 21 days, most women will become so attuned to thinking about ways to love their husband *on purpose* that it will be natural to act that way every day.

One aspect of all this is to give up our idea that if we miss one day of projects the whole thing is a failure. I know—I tend to be an all-or-nothing kind of girl, maybe a lot like you.

If you miss a day, don't beat yourself up. Just pick up again and keep going. It may take you 60 days to do 21 projects. That's OK. Just keep going.

> If the LORD delights in a man's way,
> he makes his steps firm;
> though he stumble, he will not fall,
> for the LORD upholds him with his hand.
> (Psalm 37:23-24)

Twenty-one days is just the starting point. With The Husband Project, you have a structure to work within and a goal to meet. The purpose of the 21 days is not to be able to check off the projects and be done with it, but instead, to train our minds to think about our man and consider his needs every day.

4

I've Got a Secret... and So Should You

Let me be honest with you...telling your husband about The Project is a big mistake.

This may feel counterintuitive to you. Perhaps your husband knows every little thing about you. You tell each other everything. You call each other on your lunch breaks and go over the details of your day. He knows what kind of yogurt you had this afternoon at 3:00 p.m.

Great. Still, don't tell him.

I normally would never advise any woman to keep a secret from her husband. That is just bad marriage management. Plus, it always gets you into trouble in the end. You can hide those Target bags in the back of your closet for only so long. Eventually, the Visa bill shows up in the mailbox.

But may I be so bold as to suggest The Husband Project deserves a special dispensation in your upfront, tell-all marriage relationship? Perhaps you could embrace the broader communication style of "Don't Ask; Don't Tell," only for The Husband Project, of course.

Consider this similar situation: I had a milestone birthday this year. My husband knew it was important to me that I celebrate in a big way. So for about five weeks he conspired with all my best and most creative friends to throw me a surprise party. I kinda knew something was up, but was thrilled when I walked into my friend Mary's house to 20 of my closest friends screaming, "*Surprise!*"

Yes, Roger kept a secret from me. Was I mad? Did I feel betrayed by him keeping something from me? No. My thoughts never went to, *How could you do this to me? We tell each other everything!* I felt so loved and cherished that he would take the time and the energy to go to all that trouble. He managed every detail, down to having my favorite Margherita-style pizza ready and waiting for me when I got there. I felt incredibly blessed, treasured, and honored.

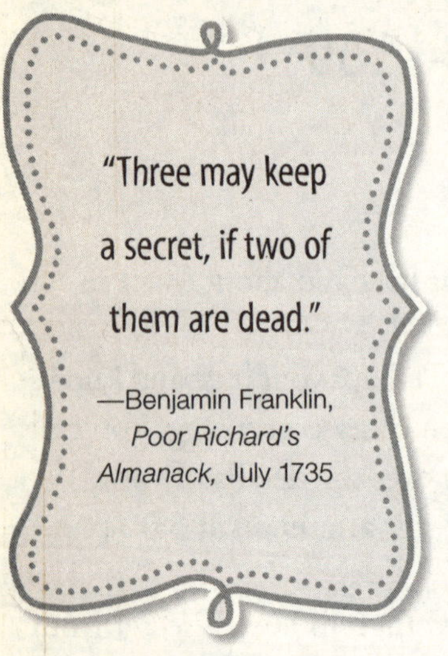

Because I knew that he had put so much time and thought into the party to make me feel oh-so-special, I remember that as one of the best days of my life.

It should be the same with The Husband Project. One of the main reasons to keep it a secret is to keep it fun. Get some of your best girlfriends to help you plan. Keep this book with you at work, in the back of your car, or hidden in the spare room he never goes into. One friend actually made a notebook with a fake cover. She called it her Home Management Journal, recognizing that if her husband was happy, she could *manage* to stay living in the same home with him.

Keep Expectations Low

If your husband knows that you're doing The Husband Project, suddenly he's going to start looking to see if you're doing things "right." We want our guys to feel honored and loved, but if he knows what's going on, it may begin to feel more like a burden to you than a blessing. You don't want to get to the point of feeling that this is one more chore to mark off your list. The idea of each project is to turn our hearts and minds toward our husbands, not to make sure that we "make it through" another marriage book.

Besides, if he discovers the Bonus Projects, that may be the only thing he looks forward to all week.

Keep It Simple

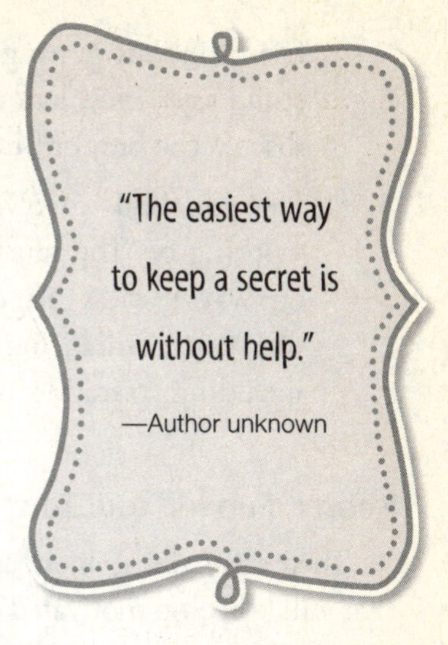

It may tip your hand if one day you barely notice when your husband gets home, and the next day you're slipping on your tiniest teddy and attacking him as he walks through the door.

The objective is not to make huge splashes in your marriage; it's to raise the level *overall.* Do something, every day, to let him know that you love him and are glad the two of you are married. When you continually look for avenues to bless him, he won't be quite so shocked (or suspicious) when it happens.

Other Ways to Keep It Undercover

- When e-mailing your accountability partners, make sure you don't use a joint account that both you and your husband log on to. You wouldn't want him to see your plans for flirty text messages, now would you? Yahoo has free e-mail accounts for the asking. Sign up at www.yahoo.com.
- Hide your calendar of activities somewhere he won't discover it. The laundry area is a safe bet in my house—no one goes there except for dire clean underwear emergencies.
- Play it cool. Don't start giggling as soon as he walks in the door and say, "Woo-hoo, have I got a surprise for you!" Make your projects a part of your everyday routine.
- Don't tell anyone else what you're doing. Loose Lips Sink Ships—and The Husband Project. Don't tell his mom, don't tell his best friend, don't tell anyone who's in regular contact with your hubby.
- Use a code word. Perhaps when you're chatting with your

friends about getting together to make your plans, you could say, "Hey, let's meet at Starbucks on Wednesday to discuss the project [the plan, the agenda]."

- Get your kids involved. No, don't tell them that you're working on The Husband Project. Just help them figure out ways to bless their dad that they can take credit for. That way, you're still loving and encouraging your husband, and including your kids in the process.

Keep It Fun for You, Too

There's something about conspiring with other like-minded women that will keep you motivated even when you're tired, grumpy, and just not getting that lovin' feeling back from your hubby. Take the extra care it will require to keep this a secret. You'll both be blessed in the process.

And If He Does Find Out

So he saw an e-mail from an accountability partner. He found this book under the front seat of the car. Oh well. Don't give up. Tell him that you're working hard on changing so that he feels more loved and appreciated. Any smart man will stop asking questions right then and just enjoy the ride.

5

Accountability: The Key to Making It Work

I'm famous for starting projects that never quite see completion. I have about $700 worth of scrapbooking materials and drawers filled with beads and fasteners, all taking up space in my home. We won't even begin to discuss the number of new-and-never-opened books I have jammed on my bookshelves (and under my bookshelves, and under my bed...).

We all have projects that we start enthusiastically and never manage to finish. Don't let this happen to you with The Husband Project.

There are several ways to assure that you stick with it for the long haul. Putting your plan on paper or jotting it in this book is one way to up your chances of doing all 21 projects. Prayer is definitely key to persisting through your project when your husband has been, let's say, less than charming that day. But by far the biggest determinant for whether you complete The Husband Project or this book gets conveniently lost under your bed is having a couple of committed accountability partners.

In the company of good friends, your experience with The Project will be more fun, more creative, and you'll increase greatly your chances of completion.

Choosing Your Project Crew

Decide on the two people you would most like to take this journey with. My suggestion is to find friends who will share a sense of adventure (or at least are willing to think outside the box a bit). Think trusted confidantes, women who can talk about lingerie and maybe even…sex! (This automatically eliminates, for most of you, your mom, his mom, daughters, and all his ex-girlfriends.)

When it came time for me to pick my partners, I spent some time thinking and praying about the women I would choose to hold me accountable. I needed women who would be fun, innovative, and willing to give me a swift kick in the behind when I began slacking. As you know, there will most likely be days when you won't want to look at your husband, much less lovingly fix a delightful little snack for him.

Location is not important. For several years, one of my accountability partners lived clear across the United States, and the other a mere four blocks away. It was challenging at first, but we made it work. E-mail was a godsend, and every once in a while, in a crisis, we would call each other. I seriously considered changing cell phone plans at one point to keep my costs down.

You may want to balance out the dynamics of your group by taking into account each woman's personality. While I'm creative and can think of 20 ways to flirt with my husband before breakfast, actually putting a plan down on a calendar is a challenge for me. That's why I need someone like my friend Angela in my life. While she's creative, her main strength is implementing; she easily puts those great ideas into action. She's the one who will e-mail me daily reminders about what surprise we've planned for our husbands each day: "It's Monday, must be back massages today!" or "Have you Bonused this week?"

Why Two Friends?

I love this story in Exodus 17:8-13 about a group of supportive friends:

> The Amalekites came and attacked the Israelites at Rephidim. Moses said to Joshua, "Choose some of our men and go out to fight the Amalekites. Tomorrow I will stand on top of the hill with the staff of God in my hands."
>
> So Joshua fought the Amalekites as Moses had ordered, and Moses, Aaron and Hur went to the top of the hill. As long as Moses held up his hands, the Israelites were winning, but whenever he lowered his hands, the Amalekites were winning. When Moses' hands grew tired, they took a stone and put it under him and he sat on it. Aaron and Hur held his hands up—one on one side, one on the other—so that his hands remained steady till sunset. So Joshua overcame the Amalekite army with the sword.

OK, so let's break this down. Moses orders Joshua to go attack the Amalekites (who were attacking them, so it seems like a perfectly reasonable thing to do). So Moses, in a show of support, goes to the top of a hill and stands there with the staff of God in his hands.

I don't know if you've ever tried to stand for a long time with something heavy over your head, but I get tired just holding my hands up at church during singing. After just a few minutes it looks like I'm doing an interpretative rendition of the "Worship Macarena"—hands up, hands down, one hand up, one hand out.

As long as Moses held his hands up, his team was winning. But whenever he lowered his hands, his team would get kicked around the field. So his guys, Aaron and Hur, climbed up the hill. And this is what I love, this is the illustration of true friendship: Those two friends came alongside Moses and not only held up his hands, but pulled up a rock so that Moses could sit down. They provided comfort and support to their friend who was standing in the battle.

As wives, there will be many circumstances where we're called to do extraordinary things for our marriage as it weathers the seasonal rough spots, unforeseen challenges, and sometimes all-out battles. It is precisely at these times that we need the support and comfort of friends who will not allow us to give up, but will, with conviction and resolve, help us stand and win when we feel overcome and overrun.

Choose these women wisely. They will get to know you and your marriage intimately. Make a commitment that when you meet (online, in your local coffee shop, wherever), what happens in your group stays in your group.

The Accountability Covenant

Once you have chosen your crew, make sure you sign the following Accountability Covenant for each other. This will give you the extra reminder of the concrete decision you have made to see The Husband Project through to the end, and your agreement to hold each other up when you feel like falling down.

Accountability will not only keep you focused and on task, it will make doing The Project a lot more fun.

The Husband Project Accountability Covenant

The Covenant

We the readers of *The Husband Project* enthusiastically agree to enter into an accountability relationship with each other for the sole purpose of engaging in and completing all projects to intentionally love and support our husbands. As accountability partners we vow to:

- hold each other accountable (even if that means a swift kick in the you-know-what)
- call each other at least three times a week
- put our plans on paper and discuss them with each other
- laugh only *with* each other, not *at* each other
- not talk badly about our husbands for the 21 days
- pray for each other every day for the 21 days
- keep details confidential—what happens in our trio stays in our trio
- ask for help, motivation, or inspiration if we're having a rough go or getting that quittin' feeling

With smiles on our faces and hope in our hearts, we sign and acknowledge "The Husband Project Accountability Covenant" this ____ day of ____________ 20___.

____
Project Manager

____
Accountability Partner

____
Accountability Partner

6

How to Handle Tough Situations during The Project

As you work through The Husband Project, no doubt some questions will come up. Here are some of the most frequent ones that keep popping up, and my best attempt to answer them.

Question 1: *Can I keep doing The Project while my husband is traveling? What about when I'm traveling? Is it better to postpone The Project until everyone is under one roof?*

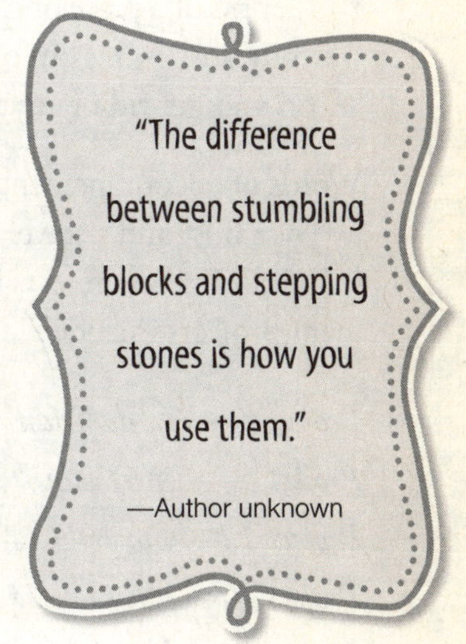

Absolutely keep going on The Project when your husband is out of town. Not every project has to be done face-to-face; in fact, some are better when you're apart. And remember, it's perfectly OK to do a project on Tuesday that he discovers when he arrives home on Saturday.

Here are ideas for how to adapt some of the projects while he's away:

Project 20—Post-it Notes, Man's Greatest Invention

- Put a Post-it in your husband's luggage so he'll find it when he unpacks.
- When you're doing his laundry, leave a love note for him to find in one of his socks.

- Leave a note on his bathroom mirror letting him know how much you missed him while he was gone and how glad you are to have him home.

Project 11—Stress-Be-Gone

- While he's traveling, make an effort to eliminate one thing that makes him crazy, without any expectation of him noticing when he gets home. Make sure he has clean clothes ready to go for the day after he gets back or fill up his gas tank before he gets back in town.

Project 15—What Not to Wear

- Get rid of a piece of clothing. This is perfect for a day when your husband is out of the house so that you can try things on and get rid of anything that either you or he hates.

Words of encouragement can be offered from any location. If you know your husband's travel schedule, it will be easy to save some of those build-him-up projects for the dates of his trip. Words of encouragement projects include:

Project 3—You da' Man

Project 5—E-flirt.com

Project 12—Gotcha! Catch Him Doing Something Great

Project 16—Is It Getting Hot in Here—Or Is It You?

Project 20—Post-it Notes, Man's Greatest Invention

Here are some creative project ideas you can do while you're the one on the road:

Project 15—What Not to Wear

- I have a few items in my wardrobe that I'd be embarrassed to share how much of an extravagance they were. The sad part is they're not necessarily my husband's favorites. While I'm traveling is a great time to wear and enjoy them without subjecting Roger to them.

Project 17—Playing Hooky

- If you have kids, arrange for one evening of babysitting while you're gone so your husband can have a couple of hours to himself.

Project 18—Dinner's on Me

- Here's a variation on kidnapping your husband and taking him out for dinner. Leave behind a gift card for him to take a friend, a kid, or even his mom out to dinner. You'll get bonus points from everyone involved (especially if your kids aren't in love with Dad's cooking).

Project 19—The Service Here Is Excellent

- Leave a secret stash of food in a basket in your bedroom. I've even put an ice bucket in our room to keep cheese cold for Roger to find.
- Do your own turndown service before you leave. (It isn't complete without the little pillow mint.)

Project 21—Car Chases and Karate Chops

- If you use Netflix or some other subscription service, arrange to have all of his testosterone-driven movies show up while you're traveling. I'm sure seeing some guy get various body parts blown to smithereens will comfort your husband in your absence.
- One time when I was going out of town, I got the latest Superman movie for Roger. I am not the biggest Superman fan, so I knew that Roger would have no guilt in watching

it without me, and I wouldn't have to suffer through it at some point in our movie-viewing future.

While it may seem like an extra burden to do The Husband Project when you or your husband travel, remember your blessing might be the little bit of encouragement he needs while he's out on the road and missing the comforts of home or you're away and he's missing you. When you know the home fires are burning, the road home doesn't seem so long.

Question 2: *What if I get sick or am just totally overwhelmed at work? Do I have to do the projects every day, or can I wait until things get a little less hectic?*

Let's be truthful. There are times when you're not going to feel like doing the projects. Life is busy, we get sick, we get tired.

The other side of the truth equation? Your life is probably not going to get any less stressful. (Really, how much easier is your life today than it was a month ago?)

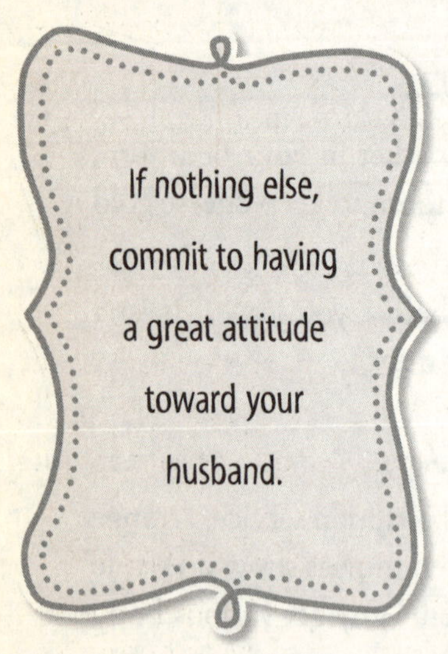

My best advice is to do what you can, plan in advance for the busy times, and if nothing else, commit to having a great attitude toward your husband. If you can do nothing else than thank him for making sure that the box of tissues is within reach while you're sick, that's what you can do at the time.

One of my friends works at a CPA's office. Yes, I would guess that April 15 would not be the best day for her to start The Project. Don't beat yourself up, or worse, abandon The Project altogether because there's been a delay.

Question 3: *Do I still do the projects when I'm fighting with my husband?*

How to handle this depends on the level of the fight.

1. I love him to pieces, but he is driving me crazy.

You fought over how to best prepare the turkey for Thanksgiving. Or, even though you asked your husband to put away the suitcases from your trip three weeks ago, there they sit by the back door.

We all get annoyed with our husbands now and then. Remember to breathe and just keep working on the projects. When I've been the most angry or frustrated with my husband, I've had to picture Jesus standing on the other side of him. I focus on loving Christ, and my husband is just standing in the way, receiving all that love.

It can be very enlightening to "love through the annoyances" and let God work on your heart. But, like most uncomfortable trials, you'll be able to truly enjoy your progress only after you're through the toughest part.

2. I don't think we will be married in another 21 days.

I've heard from several women who have fought with their husbands while doing The Project. It's amazing how issues will rise to the surface of your marriage just as you're trying to be intentional about loving your husband no matter what.

This may be the time to get some perspective from another couple you both love and respect, talk to your pastor, or get involved in some marital counseling. Perhaps the best thing The Husband Project will do for some couples is bring up those underlying issues that must be dealt with just so you can start to *like* each other again. Don't be afraid to pursue every option to make your marriage what God intended it to be.

In going through The Husband Project, many wives have come to realize that while there are real problems and difficulties with their husband that needed to be resolved, God was actually working on *their* hearts in certain areas of their marriage.

7

Every Marriage Is Different

Not every project I suggest in this book is going to be a good fit for every husband. (Hey, not every project is something *my* husband would enjoy.) My purpose for each project is to hit on the major areas where men feel loved and honored.

In one of the projects, I suggest that if there's a chore your husband hates, you could hire someone else (perhaps a neighborhood kid) to take over and get that chore off his list. My husband would love this. Most likely your husband would love it. And perhaps a few husbands might feel as if you were saying, "OK, you lazy bum. If you are not going to do it, I'll just hire someone who will." Only you know how your guy will respond, so consider his mind-set and happiness when making your plans to bless him.

There are a couple of things to be aware of while working The Husband Project:

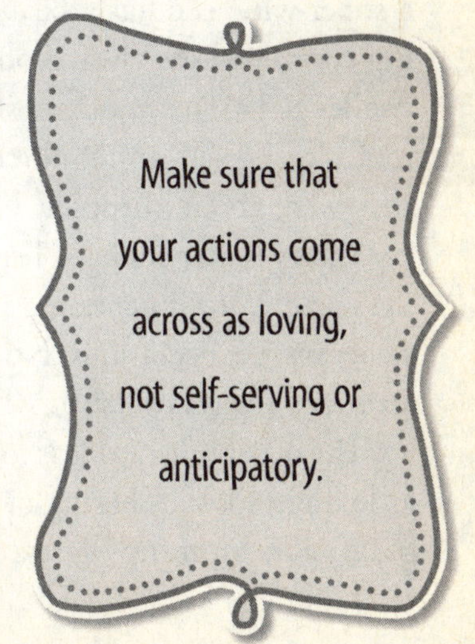

1. Check your attitude.

The main purpose of The Husband Project is not to change your husband. Really, how much success have you had in past attempts with *that* plan? Instead, it's to initiate change in yourself, your habits, and your heart.

When I do things for Roger, I need

to check myself constantly by asking, "Am I doing this to bless him, or for him to recognize me, change for me, or owe me?"

Recently, I received this e-mail from one of our project managers, Sherry:

> As the "Suzy Homemaker" type (as my friends all call me), I have always had a priority to make a nice dinner and treat my husband and family with good food. So when I received The Project e-mails about making something special in the kitchen for my husband, I thought, "Ha-ha, I already do that. I'm a step ahead of the game!"
>
> Well, I was bold and decided to share this little bit of information about myself to a good friend, who hit me with a reality check. She asked me what was my motivation for making the special food/dinner for my husband. Was it just the Suzy Homemaker in me, or was I really trying to honor and cherish my husband by making him something special? Well, as you can probably guess, my motivation has not been to treat him special. It was just a thing I already do—nothing extraordinary about it.

I love Sherry's introspection and candor. By today's standards she's a super-wife: she has a beautiful and inviting home, she's an amazing cook, and she always looks cute and well put together. But when challenged on her motives, she dug deep and realized her efforts were more for herself, to reinforce what she believed to be her role, than they were about purposely blessing her husband.

Sherry hasn't changed her actions, but after examining her motives she's being more intentional about meeting her husband's needs instead of her own expectations. No matter what we do, or how we do it, our attitudes always overshadow our actions.

The other side of this is to make sure that your actions come across as loving, not self-serving or anticipatory. I know that I can go from blessing to Mommy Martyrdom in 2.3 seconds. If I'm trying to love my guy, and I get no response for the gourmet meal or ironing his shirts, I can become bitter and resentful very quickly.

Here's the caveat: Remember that you aren't doing any of these projects to get *noticed.* If you can secretly bless your husband, even better. Make it your mission to do each project without hoping for a response. Delight in the secret satisfaction of knowing you're doing everything you can to be a blessing to your man.

2. Make the projects your own.

You're the only expert on your husband. It's up to you not to simply follow this (or any other marital program) blindly, but to tailor each project to your guy.

You're the only one who will have an inkling of whether there's an issue that would hurt your husband's feelings, bother him, or somehow annoy him. One of our project managers, Linda, knew that with Project 1 ("30 Minutes Is All It Takes: Create Some Free Time When He Gets Home") her man would not take well to being told to sit down and relax for 30 minutes. Instead, she tried to make his transition time easier by having dinner ready when he got home.

After doing several of the projects, you'll have a better understanding of what your husband most enjoys. What makes him feel supported and loved? Some guys will eat up your encouraging words, while others may need a more hands-on approach.

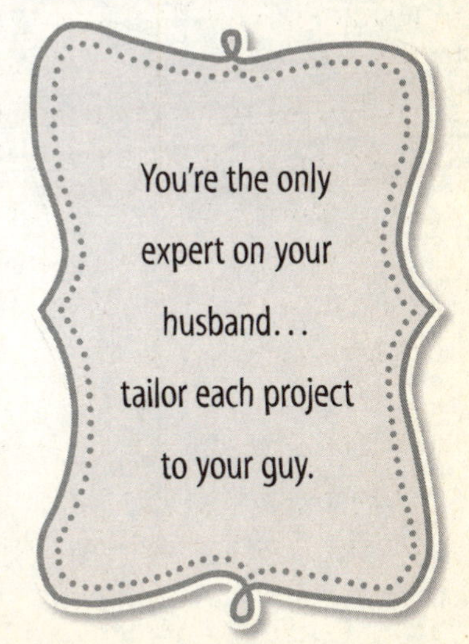

Consider this a research project of the highest importance. As you come to know what makes your husband feel cared for, you'll become more adept at adjusting each project to meet his specific needs.

These projects are designed to help you think outside of the marriage box you've built for yourself out of habit, traditions, and busyness. They're not designed to box you in. Your Project is going to look very different from your best friend's—you are married to very different guys. We're the Burger King of encouragement programs. You get to do it *your way.*

3. Make it manageable.

Maybe you and your husband are over-the-top romantics. Good for you. For the other 98 percent of us, I recommend keeping things manageable. A path of rose petals leading to you posed on a bearskin rug is great—but trying to keep up that level of blessing every night will take a toll on your life (not to mention the rug's life).

Romance like that could be a shock to your marriage system. While it's fine to mix things up once in a while, think about the temperature of your marriage. Think moderation, and kick things up just a notch or two (trade in those sweats you wear to bed for cute, matching jammies) instead of going overboard (a thong to bed may not be very sleep inducing, for either of you).

There's a subtle yet enchanting difference in letting him silently wonder, "Wow, how did I get so lucky to be married to a girl like her?" and shocking him every night with new and wild projects. Keep it simple, and then let him wonder what you're up to.

8

Looking for the Good in Your Marriage

Several years ago, during my first marriage, I went through a very rough patch in my life. I was suffering from depression in a big way, gaining huge amounts of weight, wearing black every day (not in a hip, cute way, but more of a one-step-away-from-mourning way), sleeping more and more, and generally just participating in life as little as I could get away with.

One of my good friends, Sara, had a ringside seat to my slow and painful demise. When she would call to ask me to go out for coffee, I would politely decline, stating that I was entirely too busy to be social. Actually, I was consumed with old *Friends* reruns, dreaming about a life in New York where I was a size two and had hip and clever people surrounding me.

Having a schedule to maintain (*Friends* was on four times a day), I skillfully avoided all phone calls and e-mail. That is, until Sara showed up on my doorstep and at her wit's end.

"OK, this is crazy," she said. "You are harder to get ahold of than a cloistered nun. You've *got* to rejoin society."

I looked at her blankly. "If that requires showering, count me out."

But Sara was tired of trying to keep my head above water as I kept weighing myself down. She decided to put a plan into action. She gave me a notebook and told me to start a "gratitude journal." Here were her rules:

1. Write down five things that I was grateful for every day.

2. I was not allowed to put my kids on the list (too easy).
3. I was to read the list to her every day.

I found this project (and Sara) completely annoying and stupid. Did she not see I was depressed? Why couldn't she just leave me alone?

So I did what I believed at the time was the best course of action—I hid. I used caller ID and peeked through the blinds to see who was at the door. I didn't want to practice gratitude. I was fine being miserable, thank you very much.

But Sara persisted and I relented. One day I called her and gave her what was on my list.

Kathi's List of Gratitude—July 5

1. There were no rolling blackouts today, so I could dry my hair and watch *Friends.*

"That's it?" Sara said. "For a twenty-four-hour period, all you could come up with is 'There were no rolling blackouts'?"

"Hey, it's a start, isn't it?" It really was all I could manage at the time.

Sara sighed, "OK, I want two tomorrow."

Two? She was doubling my task!

But the next day I came up with two, and by the end of the week, I had my list of five.

As I went through my day, I knew I had to find things I was grateful for. The more practice I had looking for those things, the easier it was to find them.

When I began to write down my gratitudes, my blessings started multiplying before my eyes. Things that used to make me crazy (waiting in line at the store, having to gas up my car) suddenly became little oases of gratitude. Waiting in line offered time to be still for a moment; gassing up my car gave me time to reflect on how grateful I was to have reliable transportation. My circumstances hadn't changed; only the way I looked at those circumstances was different.

Our Attitudes Determine Our Actions

In her book, *The Man You Always Wanted Is the One You Already Have,* Paula Friedrichsen discusses how we make the choice to intentionally bless our marriage:

> We get to choose how we act. Sometimes we just have to make the choice to act kind and loving regardless of how we feel. In other words, it's okay to act pleasant and joyful even when we don't feel that way. In fact, I contend that if you act pleasant and joyful long enough, you will eventually begin to feel that way…
>
> Our husbands are worthy of consistently kind and respectful treatment, and they will thrive like sunny, well-watered gardens if tended correctly. It's funny…with just a little tender loving care, men will generally respond by doing their very best to meet our needs. If we take our attention off what he's not doing right, and put our attention back where it belongs—on our own behavior—then we will find that the rest takes care of itself.

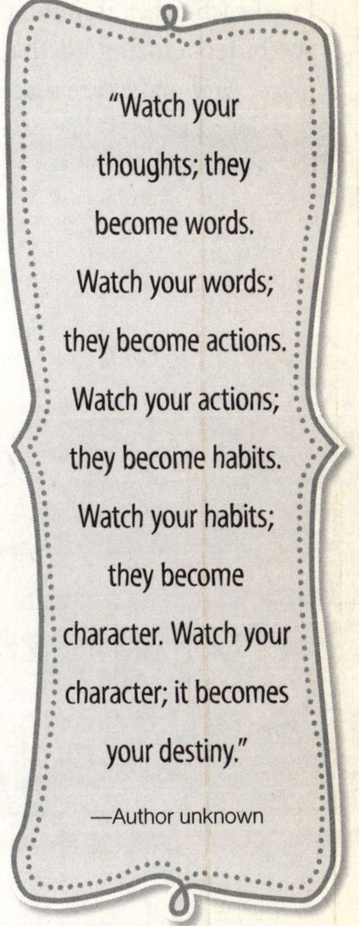

If you're having a hard time finding motivation to start some of the projects, or are just struggling with loving your husband, why not first try your own gratitude list for the 21 days? Each day, write down five things that you're grateful for when it comes to your husband. It could be tiny (he puts his cup in the dishwasher) or it could be huge (he goes to a job he doesn't love because he wants to provide for our family).

This is also great preparation for some of the upcoming projects ("You da' Man: Spreading Great Gossip about Your Guy" and others).

This is where your accountability partners can be a huge help. Hold each other accountable for your lists. Make sure that every day, you're recognizing all the reasons you married the guy in the first place. And make sure that a few regularly slip out to him so he knows how loved he is.

9

But It's Not Fair

Perhaps you've been dragged into The Husband Project by a well-meaning (i.e., pushy) friend. As you read over some of the projects, you begin to get a little uneasy. This doesn't seem like the plan for you. Either it seems weird (*Assignments to love my husband?*) or a little too Susy Homemaker (*Have a hot meal waiting for him when he gets home? I can barely get the can of Spaghettios open.*).

Then, for some wives, the first reaction certainly will be, "Hey, I work hard too! I could use a little time to myself," or "Why do I have to be the one always thinking about him? When is it his turn to think about me?"

I totally get it. I know you work hard. I do too. I bring home the bacon *and* fry it up in a pan. I work full-time, run a household, chauffeur kids to a multitude of activities, belong to a few professional organizations, and volunteer at my church. I have never eaten a bonbon or watched a soap opera in a flower-print housecoat. I truly understand being busy. But I can control only my actions, not my husband's.

After many futile attempts at self-aggrandizement, I've discovered I never seem to get anywhere in the "Hey, It's Not Fair!" game. You know the game. A special deluxe version is handed to each bride after she recites her vows and signs the marriage certificate. The rules are simple (and natural) to follow: Add up everything you do around the house, plus working, then throw a few kids into the mix, and suddenly you're ready to claim the title, Undefeated Champion of "Hey, It's Not Fair!" There are no challengers. They wouldn't dare.

So as I see it, you and I have two choices. One, we can keep playing the game, logging an ever-increasing list of resentments in our head and making ourselves and our husbands miserable. Or two, we can go counterintuitive and live a radical, Christ-like way when it comes to our marriage, putting our husband's needs before our own (or those of our kids if they're part of the picture). We can start seeing our choice to serve our husbands not as an edict or some clause in our marital contract, but as an outpouring (or in some cases, a restoring) of our love and adoration for our guys.

> "Whoever wants to become great among you must be your servant, and whoever wants to be first must be your slave—just as the Son of Man did not come to be served, but to serve, and to give his life as a ransom for many."
>
> —Matthew 20:26-28

Love and the Hockey Rink

"Scoot over closer. I'll keep you warm."

"Thanks for the sacrifice—you're such a giver," Roger mumbles with a knowing smile.

Yep, my hubby is onto me.

Whenever we're sitting together at our son's hockey game and I start to shiver, I offer to "help" my husband by snuggling up close. He gets the benefit, but so do I. It's almost always the same in serving others. While others may benefit, we're the ones who receive the biggest reward.

God instructs us to love and serve our husbands. But, in the process, God wants to do life-changing ministry *in* us. It's impossible to answer the call of Christ on your life and serve Him without being changed—becoming a little more like Christ as you serve others.

God has great things in store for His girls who are willing to put others in front of themselves. As Paul encourages us, "Let us not become weary in doing good, for at the proper time we will reap a harvest if we do not give up" (Galatians 6:9).

And here's more great encouragement from a pastor's wife after she started The Husband Project:

> I received my friend's call to participate at a perfect time. I was becoming a bit resentful and bitter over my husband's schedule—he has been very busy with his work and ministry. I have been praying that he would "hear from God" and be willing to change jobs and even change churches, but this project is changing my attitude towards him and his work. I realize that I had become caught up in my daily responsibilities and have failed to be "purposeful in loving and supporting him." I can say that I am enjoying the work in progress and Hubby has been responsive. He's been more positive, open, and has even made it home a couple of times in between work and rehearsals. Thanks again.

While it's obvious that her husband is reaping the benefits of The Project, it's also apparent that the biggest blessing here is the one our friend is receiving—peace about her situation and a new attitude toward her man.

When we lay aside our rights, those things we "deserve" as a wife, this gives our husbands, and our God, a bigger opportunity to bless us.

10

Glossary of Terms

Project

A provided activity by which you'll bless your guy, making him feel special, loved, appreciated, adored, admired, honored, or pampered... and if he's really lucky, all of the above! There are 21 *Projects* in all.

Project Manager

Head cheerleader for the "make my guy feel great" campaign. That would be you! You're already queen of the house, the proverbial belle of the ball, and now, since you're the one taking charge on each and every project, *you're* the *Project Manager.*

Accountability Partner

Someone who helps keep your feet to the fire—The Husband Project fire, that is. *Accountability Partners* (two of them) join you in this project to collectively discuss your plans and goals, provide enthusiasm, inspiration, and maybe a little laughter along the way.

Bonus Projects

Sex. Yep, that's what the *Bonus Projects* are all about. Sex, plain and simple. You'll be finding ways to physically bless your man at least once a week for each of the three weeks. No doubt these projects will be some of your guy's favorites, and hopefully some of yours as well.

Lingerie

An essential part of any *Project Manager's* tool kit. In the article,

"The Real Woman's Guide to Lingerie Shopping," (found in the Tools of The Husband Project section at the back of this book) we give you all the good stuff you need to know to make a splash with a little sex appeal and a lot of self-confidence.

Guy Food

Recipes we've provided (also in the Tools section) so you can bless your guy, regardless of your culinary skills. Think comfort food. Think rich, yummy, oooey-gooey, creamy, cheesy, and generally doctor-restricted. You won't find these dishes on the low-fat, low-carb menus, but you will find them at the top of your husband's favorite foods list.

Guy Movies

Manly movie fare recommended by guys I actually know. Movie categories include sports, action, comedy, and, of course, gratuitous violence. Meet your man's need for speed, greed, and the occasional backhanded deed. As a courtesy, there's a short list of movies-for-two for you both to enjoy together.

Project Reports

Some of the earliest *Project Managers* put The Husband Project to the test and gladly shared some of their success stories. Not only are they entertaining to read, but you can find some inspiring ideas too. *Project Reports* are highlighted at the end of each *Project.*

Getting Creative

Unique, fresh, and specific ideas—just what you need to help you complete each *Project.* Sometimes the hardest part in running the race is getting off the starting block. To help you over this potential hurdle each *Project* features a *Getting Creative* section to get you motivated and mobilized to bless your man.

Building Him Up

Launching The Husband Project

The Send-Off

Congratulations! I am very excited that you've made a commitment to become an expert in your own marriage.

There are going to be some days when The Husband Project is going to be hard to complete. Kids are needy, your job is stressful, and running around for the right kind of Ben and Jerry's ice cream is going to seem overwhelming (and a little silly).

My prayer is that you don't become discouraged. Your husband is worth it, you are worth it, and your marriage is worth it.

Your husband is worth it, you are worth it, and your marriage is worth it.

My prayer for you (as it is for my own marriage) is found in 2 Thessalonians 3:5:

May the Lord direct your hearts into God's love and Christ's perseverance.

God has great things in store for your marriage. Have loads of fun discovering (or rediscovering) them.

Kathi

Week One Projects

Project 1

30 Minutes Is All It Takes

Create Some Free Time When He Gets Home

"There's never enough time to do all the nothing you want."

Bill Watterson, "Calvin and Hobbes"

Your Project

Focus on your husband's transitional 30 minutes today. Would he like to be left alone to rest and rejuvenate, or does he want some undivided attention from you? The point is to let your husband know you value what he does out in the world, and that he has a safe, loving place to come home to and get refreshed at the end of the day.

OK, so I may be dating myself here. Growing up, I couldn't wait to watch *Mr. Rogers' Neighborhood.* Although, I have to admit, the Neighborhood of Make Believe completely freaked me out.

I think what I loved about Mr. Rogers was his gentle demeanor, but if you ask me what I remember most about the show, it would definitely be his "getting home" routine. I loved his ritual of changing from his work clothes into his at home duds. His transition each day marked the end of his time *out there* in the world and the beginning of the more relaxing, comfortable time. There was something reassuring about knowing that he was ready to focus on being home.

There's something inside your husband that craves that transition. Most men need some way *to signal the end of work and the beginning of home*—lying down for a little bit, reading a magazine, going to their cave (bedroom, garage, computer), or yes, maybe by changing into their favorite colonial cardigan and tennis shoes.

Welcome Home, Honey—Now Take the Kids

How do you greet your husband at the end of a long day? Do you encourage a little world-to-cave time for your guy?

Are you home first? If you stay at home, or get through the door before he does, do you meet him with a list of things that needs to be done, a list of complaints about your day, or perhaps an armful of kids?

If he's there when you get there, do you blow through the door with a list of activities for the rest of the night that would rival any cruise director?

Most men are looking for just a few minutes to transition from work to home. Focus on his transition tonight. If you have kids, let them give Dad a quick hug and tussle. If it's the two of you, give him a kiss and then let him know that he's off duty for the next half hour. You have things under control. He can lie down, watch TV, read a book, play a video game—whatever. The choice is his.

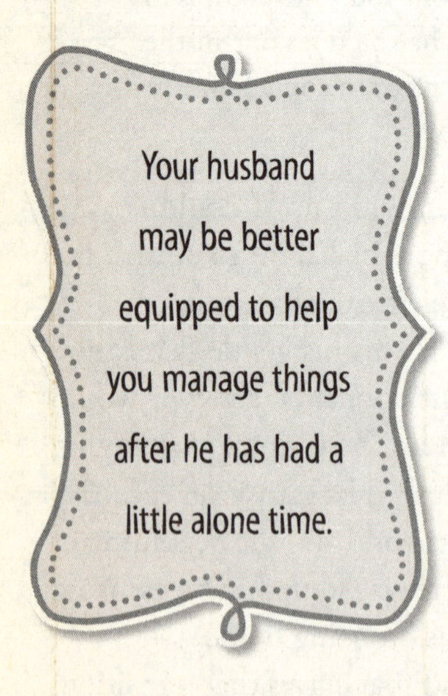

Plus, your husband may be better equipped to help you manage things after he has had a little alone time. In fact, in our very scientific study here at The Husband Project, there was a sudden increase in men doing dishes after being given a bit of free time.

Think about it. I know that I can get completely frazzled being caught in commuter traffic after a long day. All I want to do is crawl under the covers and hide from the world. Then, after a few minutes of quiet, I become fit company again. I am ready to be a useful member of society and drastically less inclined to snap at members of my family who, after several years of fruitless training, have not yet discovered that the guest bathroom floor is not an appropriate place to drop your backpack. (But I digress.)

Our husbands are out there in the world, dealing with people who may not always be the most delightful company. Our guys need to know that while the world may be a hard and tiresome place, they can rely on us, their wives, to be that soft place to land at the end of the day.

Different Husbands, Different Needs

While some husbands would love a few minutes of peace when they cross the threshold, some men would love nothing more than for you to ask about their day—and then have you actually listen to their answer.

Some husbands want to connect with their wives for their 30 minutes (different guys, different needs). Listen to how Project Manager Cheri used her husband's transitional time to meet their unique circumstances:

> My situation is a little bit different, as I'm the full-time worker in the family and my husband is at home most of the time. So at the end of the day, he usually isn't looking for cave time—he's usually had quite a bit of it, as our kids are in high school.
>
> So I translated this assignment into "30 minutes of what's important to him right now." That meant I did *not* give him a 30-minute answer to his loving question, "So, how was your day?" I gave him the 30-second summary and then asked, "Tell me about *your* day."
>
> Since he's been unemployed for over a year, I know it's important for him to list everything he's done to benefit the family, as he feels "unmanly" that he doesn't generate income. Personally, I don't *care* how many loads of laundry got done or

> how long the grocery shopping took...but I'm thrilled that he did it!
>
> After about 10-15 minutes of this, we just hung out in his home office/music studio while he showed me the latest musical stuff he's been doing. (This was hard for me because I am not a "hang out" kinda gal—I'm a go, go, goer!)
>
> He seemed so much happier than usual the rest of the evening, more connected, and it even seemed to make him more patient while helping our daughter with Algebra II!

This may take a lot of self-control on your part, but ask, and then listen—actively listen and ask questions—without complaining or one-upping him. Just listen.

Homecomings—What's the Vibe of Your Home?

Here are just a couple areas to think about when looking at your husband's transition time. Do you have:

- classical music playing softly in the background
  or
  kids performing the theme song to *Dora the Explorer* on your Pampered Chef pots and pans?
- dinner simmering away in the Crock-Pot
  or
  you're the one simmering because you have to figure out what to fix for dinner—again?
- the soft glow of scented candles around the living room
  or
  the soft glow of *Oprah* from the plasma TV?

Try walking in the door of your home and see what you notice as you cross the threshold. What's the vibe that your house gives off? Does your home give you a hug or a panic attack?

If this seems like a lot of work for the first project, just remember, this little activity is a gift for both of you. Taking some effort to work on your husband's transition time will only make your home a more warm and loving place for both of you.

Make it a priority to build that soft place to land into his evening.

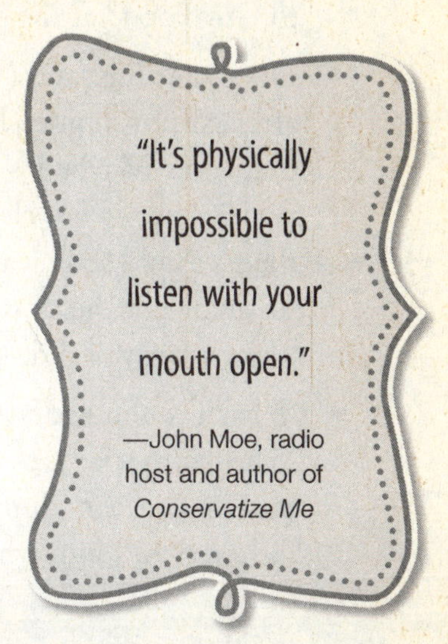

Prayer for Today

Dear God, help me to drop the to-do list for my husband today and focus on who he is, not just what he can do.

Getting Creative

There are plenty of reasons why it might not be easy for you to give your husband some transition time at the end of the day. You need to look at what can work for *your* relationship. Be creative, as in the stories listed below. Brainstorm with your friends until you find an arrangement that will work for you and your guy.

- My friend, Joann, purposely scheduled her daughter's dance classes twice a week at the same hour that her husband gets home from work. That way, her hubby comes home to an empty house. He gets some quiet, and she gets a more peaceful man.
- One husband has his workshop out in the garage. His wife encourages him to hang out there for a while before dinner. (Since starting this arrangement, her husband has started helping out with the after-dinner cleanup. Nice side benefit.)
- Crock-Pots are The Husband Project's best friend. Set your Crock-Pot to be finished 30 minutes after your husband gets home from work. Let him know that you don't need

anything until dinner is ready. Don't know a Crock-Pot from a flowerpot? Check out the recipes in "A Chick's Guide to Guy Food" at the end of this book.

- Does your husband already have a great transition routine after getting home? Find some other little thing to bless that time. Maybe it's making sure the TV is available, his favorite sweats are clean and ready to be changed into, or there's a cold soda waiting for him in the fridge. It may be so small that he doesn't even notice. That's okay—you'll know what you did.
- What if your husband works from home? Maybe the best way to help him relax is to ask what he would like the schedule to be. Does he want dinner before or after he gets some time to recharge? Ask him what would make his evening better.

Project Reports

"I did the first assignment of giving my husband 30 minutes of time to himself. When I told him to take 30 minutes to do something to relax, he looked at me, puzzled, and said, 'MOPS (Mothers of Pre-Schoolers) really brainwashed you or something! What's the catch?' Then I told him there was no catch, and he looked at me weird again and said, 'Really? I would like that.' Then he spent time shopping online for books he's been wanting to get. So it went well. And it was so fun to see his reaction!"—Christina

"Usually when my husband gets home it's a pretty crazy time of the day for me and our kids. It's dinner time and the kids are getting hungry and fussy and so am I. Trying to get a dinner together is the hardest thing for me to do, so when my husband walks through the door, he usually sees us all a little frazzled and jumps in to help. (He's a much better cook than I am.) I decided today to make soup ahead of time, so it was already done when he got home. I could focus on him, and he didn't feel compelled to help me finish cooking. It was a much more relaxed atmosphere, and I plan to use the Crock-Pot a lot too!"—Dawn

"What I found out is that when I get home from work my husband wants a little time from me. So instead of coming in and immediately changing my clothes and going to my computer to check e-mail, I gave him my time. And you know what was so cute? He had done the grocery shopping that day, and he wanted to show me the things he had purchased and explain why he made some of the choices he had made. He also showed me some articles in the paper that he thought I would be interested in. As of immediately, I will be changing my routine when I first get home from work and give my guy my time."—RMK

"I try to give my husband a few minutes of down time when he walks in the door. He works with kids all day long. So after the initial 'Daddy, Daddy' when he walks in the door, he goes somewhere quiet to decompress, then comes out ready for the craziness of dinner time."—Moanie

Your Plan for the Project *(copy your plan on The Husband Project Planner at the back of this book)*

Your Results *(his reaction, my reaction, etc.)*

Project 2

Back in the Day

Do Something He Enjoyed Before You Got Married

"Lust is easy. Love is hard. Like is most important."

Carl Reiner

Your Project

Initiate an activity that your husband used to love. Whether it's his favorite hobby, sport, or pastime, it's time for you to get involved. Be his buddy today.

Most guys don't spend a lot of time hanging out with their buddies—*you* are his buddy. He married you to have a built-in friend who he can do all those fun things with. (The fact that the two of you can have sex is definitely a bonus.)

It's vital for men to build friendship into their lives, and as wives, we have a responsibility to encourage our guys to hang out with other good guys. However, in most marriages, our husbands will be looking to us to do life with.

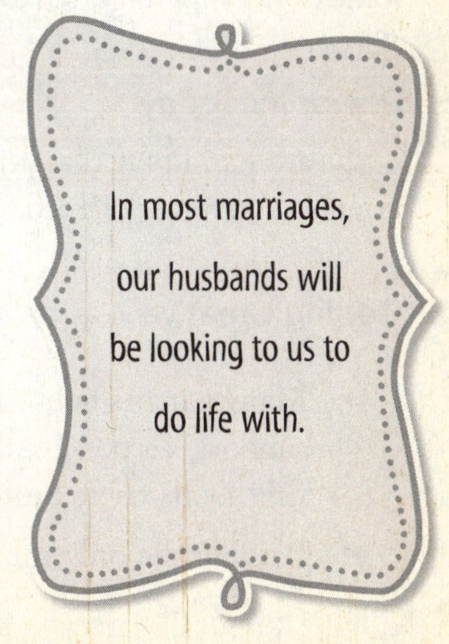

My husband loves to go to the woods, build a fire, and have a cookout. I'm more of a white tablecloth kind of girl. But, you *know* while we were dating

I was the happiest "camper" around. I prepared the food for our open flame. I bought cute hiking boots. I joined him on seemingly endless hikes surrounded by mosquitoes and poison oak. While we were dating, I would have hunted wild moose just to be with him.

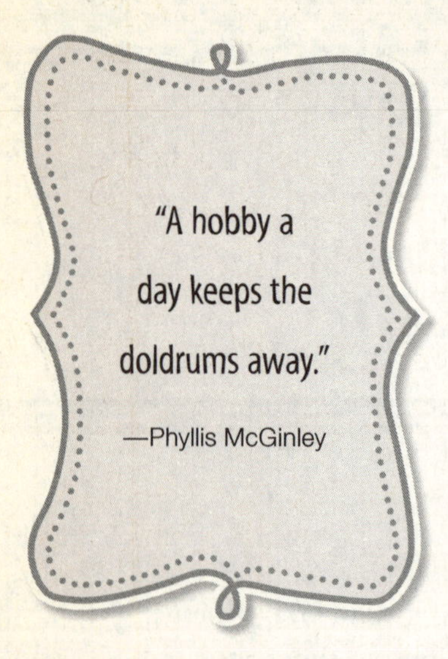

Once we were married, many of my husband's favorite activities were put on the back burner...I would love to be able to say that I encouraged him to have his "guy time," but there was a house to clean, kids to raise, and jobs to get to. Watching all six *Star Wars* movies and trekking into the mountains would have to wait until our kids were grown (and possibly until early retirement).

It's time to think about those things your husband loves to do with you, his buddy. Maybe it's hiking up a mountain, hanging out at Best Buy, or watching his alma mater's football team. It doesn't matter if you like it or not—your fun will come from watching the look on your husband's face as he reclaims some of his long forgotten loves. (Video gaming anyone?)

Prayer for Today

Dear God, I pray that my husband can view me as his friend and lover, as You have designed.

Getting Creative

- Many a man's hobby has gone by the wayside due to matrimony. Is it possible that it's time you learned to golf or fly fish? Don't try to beat him, just join him.
- Possibly the only thing your husband would enjoy more

than playing chess with you is teaching you how to play chess (or whatever activity he's interested in). Ask for a lesson so he can teach you something that he is an expert at (or really loves). Just your willingness to learn will be a huge boost to your guy.

- Pick up a magazine about your guy's now dormant hobby. Ask him questions about why he loves it so much. Learn a couple of technical terms so that you are better able to discuss it.
- Do a little research. Find out what the definitive website is for your husband's favorite subject. Maybe there's an event in town, a lecture to attend, or a game to watch.

Project Reports

"My husband is a public school principal. He is great at what he does, but the job is taxing emotionally. We have two children, a sixteen-year-old daughter and a nine-year-old son. They both want his attention, and he spends a lot of time with them. He also has a wife who has her own set of needs. All that said, there is not a lot of time for him.

"When I plan something that I know he will really like—a hike on a beautiful trail, something we did a lot more of pre-kids—his face lights up. A heaviness is lifted from him and he begins to look at maps and Google Earth. He is completely into the adventure before him. It is fun to see him get so joyful over the thought of taking a hike, of all things. I love pleasing him that way."—Sue

"Watching sports on television was definitely something my husband enjoyed before we were married. Sports bar 'dates' with the guys during football season were pretty common. Now, ten years later, all the buddies have become dads themselves and are too busy to enjoy watching games away from home. When football comes on the TV at home, I usually head for another part of the house in search of a project to keep me busy for a couple of hours. Nothing better than going out shopping on Super Bowl Sunday—the stores are empty! Last week I stayed put and watched a game with him and the boys. A couple of times during the game my husband had to leave the room to take calls from work. He was so surprised to come back into the room each time to 1) find the TV still on (I usually turn it off), 2) the channel hadn't been changed (the kids usually put on cartoons), and 3) I knew the score! Brownie points for me."—SL

"My husband used to scuba dive, but he hurt his ears and can no longer do that. I asked him about a hike with me and the kids, and he *loved* the idea. It was *four* hours and a pretty strenuous hike. I had our toddler on my back for at least a good three-fourths of the time for safety reasons. My 11-year-old loved every minute of it, and we brought plenty of food and water. We all enjoyed the great outdoors, and it's something I know we as a family need to do more often."—BB

Your Plan for the Project *(copy your plan on The Husband Project Planner at the back of this book)*

Your Results *(his reaction, my reaction, etc.)*

Project 3

You da' Man

Spreading Great Gossip about Your Guy

"It isn't what they say about you, it's what they whisper."

ERROL FLYNN

Your Project

Say something nice about your husband to someone else. Make sure you tell him what you said, and to whom.

As cliché as it may sound, our husbands want to be our heroes. More than they want to know that we love them, they want to know that we respect them. They need to know that they're never the butt of our jokes, that they're the go-to-guy in every story we tell.

Make an opportunity today to brag on your husband to someone else. It doesn't matter if it's one of your friends or one of his; let that somebody know how blessed you are to be married to your guy. Some key phrases you may want to put on index cards to help you remember:

- "I feel so lucky to have a man who knows how to do his own laundry."
- "You know when I knew that my husband really loved me? When he could remember my order at Starbucks."
- "I just love the way he is with our kids."
- "He makes the best lasagna on the planet."

Steering the Ship

The Book of James contains this warning about the power of our tongues: "A small rudder on a huge ship in the hands of a skilled captain sets a course in the face of the strongest winds. A word out of your mouth may seem of no account, but it can accomplish nearly anything—or destroy it" (James 3:3-4 MSG).

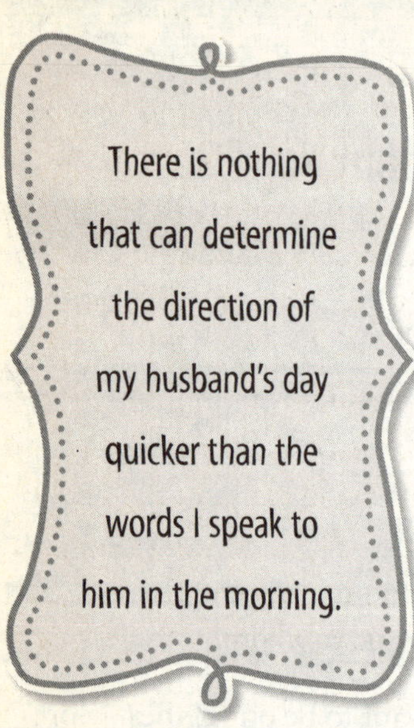
There is nothing that can determine the direction of my husband's day quicker than the words I speak to him in the morning.

As wives, we are often the ship's captain, while our husbands are the huge ship. Words spoken in encouragement and love can go a long way to building our men up. But the opposite is true as well. There is nothing that can determine the direction of my husband's day quicker than the words I speak to him in the morning.

Sometimes as wives, we forget the role we play in our husband's lives. We all remember that great line from *My Big Fat Greek Wedding,* spoken by Toula's mom: "The man may be the head of the household, but the woman is the neck. She tells him which way to turn."

OK, I don't tell my husband which way to turn, but I do have an influence about how he navigates through his day. I know that I need to be especially careful about my tone. Sometimes I think I am just oh-so-witty, when really I come off as sarcastic and biting.

It's not enough to just say kind and encouraging words. I need to make sure that whatever words I choose only build up my husband, never tear him down.

Death to the Dufus Dad

Our world encourages us to define our husbands by what is lacking in them. Need proof? Just turn on your TV. Watch any channel for more than ten minutes and you're almost assured of seeing some man playing the role of the dufus dad. You know the one: his wife is always right, his kids don't respect him, and he's the punch line of every joke, accompanied by a laugh track. Even his best friend, the dog, thinks he's a moron.

I feel like it's time for a man revolution in our generation. No, I don't want to go back to the times where women were tethered to the oven by their ever-present strand of pearls. But I do want to see a place where men are allowed to be men *and* they can be respected for it.

My warrior cry will be, "Death to the Dufus Dad!" But I digress.

OK, so you've bragged on your husband. Now what?

Once you've done your bragging, let your husband know what you said and to whom you said it. He needs to know that he is the good guy in every story you tell.

With the tone of our speech, we can have a lot of influence over our friends. Here's how my friend, Michelle, puts it when it comes to steering away from complaining about her husband, Rick:

> I love this project and have practiced it for years, even when I was irritated with my husband. Sometimes hearing yourself point out the good stuff gives you the power to change your own perception of something that's annoying—of course, not that Rick is *ever* annoying.
>
> Another thing I think about...how women can help other women. When a woman is complaining about her husband (not confiding, because I think there's a difference and we should be there for our buddies), but when it's a lighthearted complaint, where a friend may be stuck in a rut, thinking about something in regard to her husband, I try and gently encourage her to see the goodness in her husband. I might say something like, "Yeah, he likes to watch football, but think of how he's also bonding with your sons by sharing something they have in common!" I try to find the silver lining and "illuminate" that for my friend.

While your greatest need may be for your husband to tell you that he loves you, most guys are programmed differently. He wants, at his very core, to know that you respect him. He wants to know that you are proud of him and that he is the one you would choose again if given the chance.

This goes a long way to solidifying you as a team, as well. There's no way that anyone in my family would ever say a word against my husband. They know that I'm on his side, and it's a gossip-free zone around me (unless the gossip is about how great he is).

Prayer for Today

Dear God, let the words of my mouth and the meditations of my heart be acceptable in Your sight.

Getting Creative

Who are the important people in your husband's life? Your kids, his parents, his friends? Be intentional about who you chat with when you brag on him; it's almost as important as actually doing it.

Having a hard time coming up with something? I still brag on my guy for things he did years ago. He loves when I tell the story of how brilliantly he proposed (there were waterfalls and stuffed portobello mushrooms involved).

Here are some other areas to think about when crafting your brag:

- His parenting skills
- His patience level
- The way he treats your mom
- His culinary ability
- His job
- His loyalty to you

Project Reports

"This last Valentine's Day my husband, Guy, did wonderful

things for our children and for me. I had the opportunity to brag about these things to my sister on my cell phone with my husband right there. If you're wondering what he did, he made up a treasure hunt for each of our three children. They each had three clues before they got their prize, and he made each of the clues rhyme. The kids absolutely *loved* it, and I was very impressed as well. For myself, I have a mother/daughter date with my eldest daughter every Thursday night, and we didn't get home until about 9:30 p.m. He had a bunch of candles lit in our bedroom, wonderful coupons for me to use for time away from the kids, not to make dinner, and more. There was also champagne, Barry White playing on the CD, and chocolates. The *best* Valentine's Day ever!"—Carolyn

"I made a decision long ago (before I was even married, oddly enough) to try not to say negative things about my husband to other people. I have heard lots of wives complain about their husbands, and I realized that it not only makes the person talking feel bad (continuing to think about the negative), but it also makes the listener feel bad (caught in between and *never* knowing the right thing to say). I admit it's not easy, and I do have moments when all I want to do is vent. But I really try hard to stick to the 'if you don't have something nice to say…' rule."—Becky

"The bragging was easy for me. It just so happened that I had my two-year-old's b-day party that day. Boy oh boy did everyone there get an earful of what a big help my husband was for helping me with the party."—Michelle

"Okay, so I kinda cheated on this one. We were talking about this project at MOPS, so I said to the ladies at my table, 'Just so ya know, my husband is awesome!' So it was a little contrived, but I totally meant it. I'll keep working at this assignment though. I want to make a habit of saying nice things about my husband in a more natural way."—Christina

"I, too, try not to disparage my husband in front of other people (or to him for that matter), but I think I had gotten lazy about talking him up. He is a fabulous man, and this week I made a point to let people know. My sweet hubby was a little embarrassed, but he beamed when I told him about it. It feels great to focus on his strong points. It reminds me why I love him even more now than when I married him!"—Stacie

Your Plan for the Project *(copy your plan on The Husband Project Planner at the back of this book)*

Your Results *(his reaction, my reaction, etc.)*

Project 4

Heart vs. Stomach

A Treat Just for Him

"There is no sincerer love than the love of food."
George Bernard Shaw

Your Project

Get a food treat for your husband that he's not required to share with you or any other family member.

It's time to think about food, glorious food.

My husband goes positively bonkers over a candy called Cherry Sours. He was first introduced to this candy during his Florida childhood (which, from what I can tell, was spent largely at Walt Disney World), and he has great memories associated with it. The candy in question is a little red sugar ball, and my guy is desperately, inexplicably in love with mass quantities of them.

Which totally confounds me. They taste like the stuff your dental hygienist uses to rinse your mouth out after a painful and thorough cleaning.

But he loves 'em, so I search for Cherry Sours whenever I can. They can be hard to find, so when I do, I stock up without Roger knowing. When he's having a rough time at work or I want to say congratulations for a job well done, I break out the Cherry Sours.

Is there a treat that you find revolting but your husband absolutely loves? Get it for him, letting him know through this small act, "This is all for you, baby" (and if you truly don't like the treat, he won't feel obligated to share).

Even if you do love it, insist that it's all for him. Don't let him share with you. This is something special that does not require him to share with his neighbor. (It's perfectly acceptable to get a matching treat for yourself.)

Prayer for Today

Dear God, I want my husband to know that he is honored and cherished, even in the little things I do for him.

Getting Creative

Stumped for ideas? Here are some thoughts:

- Get his favorite pint of Ben & Jerry's and hide it behind the frozen chicken, ready and waiting for his special night.
- Is there a certain cut of meat your husband loves? How about having the butcher cut something just for him. Most supermarkets will even do the marinade for you, giving you one less thing to think about.
- Is there a certain candy your husband loves from his childhood? Check out www.candywarehouse.com. They have all the nostalgic candy you could want (Black Jack Gum, anyone?) while also carrying any modern favorite you could be looking for.
- My husband's family loves something called "noodles and mashed potatoes" (we lovingly refer to it as "The Starch Fest"). I learned how to make this special dish just for him.

- My guy loves the smell of baking almost as much as he enjoys eating the treat. Have some brownies in the oven when he gets home from work or working out. (I know it negates the workout, but isn't chocolate always worth it?)
- Our friend Scott mentioned that he loves cranberry sauce, but gets to eat it only at Thanksgiving. His wife made the holiday treat for him this past July.
- Are you a wife who is an expert at low-cal salads and other forms of chick-food? Check out "A Chick's Guide to Guy Food" at the back of this book for some manly inspiration.

Project Reports

"My lactose intolerant husband loves soy ice cream (yuck), and he has run out of his favorite kind that we can get only at a certain market in town. So...today I will make a trip to the market on the other side of town and pick up some Chocolate Peanut Butter Soy Dream Ice Cream. And he can eat *all* of it."—Marci

"Easiest project so far! Pace Picante salsa *hot* with tortilla chips, plus a run to KFC for hot wings. I love that this project coincided with 'Big Game' day. It made my day to love on him with his favorite football snacks."—Karmyn

"I actually combined two days in one today. I was my husband's buddy and watched the Seahawks–Packers game with him. I had a pretty strong feeling about how that would turn out! I was right, so after the game I ran out and got him a pint of his favorite Ben & Jerry's ice cream. It was extra special for him because we have been on a diet, and he hasn't been eating many of his favorite foods. I wasn't sure how I would fit the favorite food day in. That worked, and it helped ease his pain over our team's *big loss!*"—Denise

"I am going on a scrapbooking retreat, so I thought I would

leave him one of his favorite treats and leave little sweet notes around the house for him to find while I'm gone."—SB

"I put the dark chocolate bar that he got for Christmas in a special place in the refrigerator and told him it was there and that I wouldn't eat any of it. He's the type that will eat just a little piece from it and make it last for a long time. I would've devoured it by now!"—RMK

Your Plan for the Project *(copy your plan on The Husband Project Planner at the back of this book)*

Your Results *(his reaction, my reaction, etc.)*

Project 5

E-flirt.com

Text or E-mail Some Sweet Nothings

"I turn on my computer. I wait patiently as it connects. I go online. My breath catches in my chest until I hear three little words, 'You've got mail.' I hear nothing, not a sound on the streets of New York. Just the beat of my own heart...I have mail, from you."

MEG RYAN AS KATHLEEN KENNEDY IN *You've Got Mail*

Your Project

Send a flirty text or e-mail to your husband.

I remember when Roger and I were first dating how desperate I was to get a phone call, a text message, or an e-mail from him. We lived more than 125 miles apart, and since we were both single parents, our Monday through Friday communication was always via our cell carrier. I could not wait to see his name come up on my little phone screen. My heart would skip a beat just to think that he was somewhere, out there, thinking about me and wanting to be with me.

Then real life happened. We got married, moved our families together, had kids to nurture, a mortgage to pay, laundry to fold, and lasagna to bake. There was a point where neither of our hearts had risen above a waltz, much less gotten to a mambo.

Several months after we got married, I realized that just because I got to see my husband every day, that was no reason to give up letting him know I was thinking about him. That's when the barrage of flirty text messages began flying back and forth, and that's when we started having some fun.

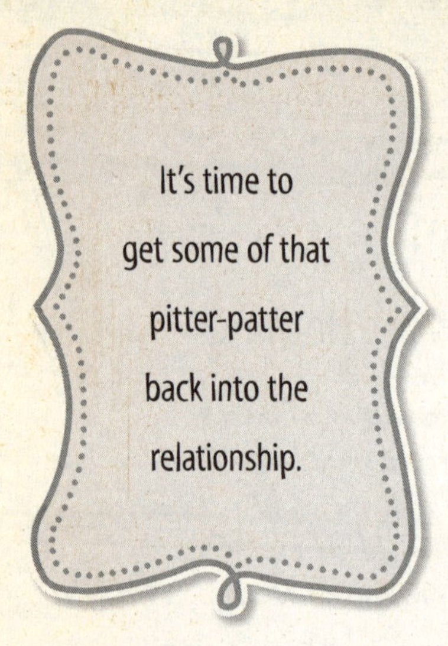

I sent one on a Tuesday morning, just letting him know that I already missed him and couldn't wait until I got to see him at dinner. I received an unusually quick reply, letting me know that he wholeheartedly agreed.

Success.

Maybe like us, it's time to get some of that pitter-patter back into the relationship.

Send your husband a flirty e-mail or text message today. Let him know you cannot wait to see him tonight—that you are counting the hours. A little over the top? I bet he won't think so.

If you're going to go beyond flirty to slightly scandalous (which, by the way, I highly encourage) make sure it's his private e-mail or cell phone. You don't want Big Brother at his company knowing how little you'll be wearing tonight.

Prayer for Today

Dear God, may my husband have the security to know that he's the only man for me—that You have designed us to be together.

Getting Creative

- Use an e-card service (hallmark.com or americangreetings .com) to send a cute and flirty note.
- Don't know how to text? Ask any teenager in the general vicinity.
- Most phones have a camera feature where you can send a photo message. Be sure to keep it G-rated so that he doesn't get in trouble at work.

Project Reports

"I truly did not think this would work. My husband wouldn't even know how to read a text message, and he rarely checks his e-mail. But we had a fight this last weekend, and I wasn't so nice. So I sent him an online greeting card apologizing and letting him know I love him. The day after I sent the card, we ended up meeting for lunch. I didn't say a word about the card. As we were leaving, we approached his car first and he got in. I leaned over to give him a kiss, and he had that cute little schoolboy grin on his face. And he said 'Thanks for the card.' That look was worth a million bucks."—RMK

"I texted him on my break at work today. It was sweet and sexy. He was more shocked that I would text him than the fact that I made sexual advances! I know he enjoyed the flirting, but all he said was that I tired him out last night (I did the Bonus Project the night before). He was just kidding, but I think he was partially serious."—SB

"I sent him a text the day before, but since it went so well that time I decided to do it again. He loved the dialog and the special note just for him."—LJ

"Usually phone calls or text messages from home involve, 'What time are you leaving work today? Can you stop by the store...' or 'Your child did this today. You need to have a talk with him/her when you get home!' So I wasn't too hip to text or call my husband during work hours if I could help it. I wanted to give him a break from all that during this 21-day project. My lack of pestering him during his work day has resulted in him calling home, *just because.* Nice change!"—SL

"A few weeks ago my husband, Bill, was in Japan. In an e-mail he sent, something he said struck me funny, even though what he said wasn't funny. But I just sensed that God spoke to me and said, 'Flirt with your husband; he needs it.' I haven't flirted with him, probably, since we got married.

(You can still have fun and enjoy each other without flirting.) Oh, it was fun, made me feel young again. He never said anything, but I'm sure it put a smile on him. I'm going to keep this up."—PGK

Your Plan for the Project *(copy your plan on The Husband Project Planner at the back of this book)*

Your Results *(his reaction, my reaction, etc.)*

Project 6

A Little Hands-on Attention

Meeting Your Husband's Physical (Touch) Needs

"When you touch a body, you touch the whole person, the intellect, the spirit, and the emotions."

JANE HARRINGTON

Your Project

> Do something to help your husband enjoy physical touch. Find something that will help him relax. New pillows, massage lotions, a back rub...your choice. Make it something that both of you will enjoy.

What does your husband consider relaxing?

Here's the project where you get to choose between Thai, Indian, and Moroccan; learn about choosing and blending oils; and get elbow-deep in the technique of kneading. Nope, it's not watching the Food Channel together. It's all about massage.

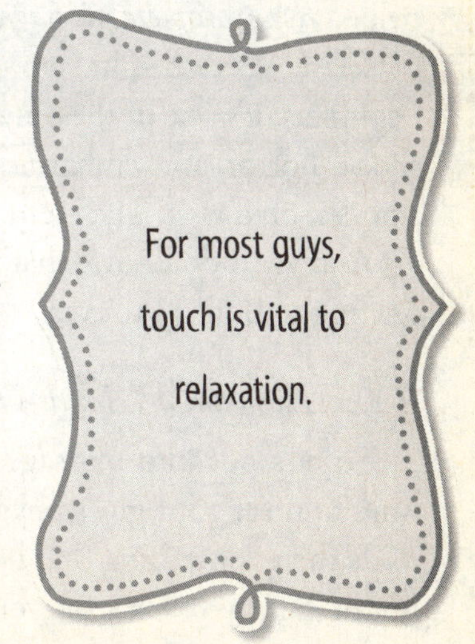

Remember when you were dating how hard it was to keep your hands off each other? Fortunately, Roger and I had excellent chaperones (four teenage kids) while we were engaged. I remember thinking, "I cannot wait to be married so we can actually be alone and do all this hugging and kissing and..."

After a few years of marriage, however, I seem to have developed excellent self-control.

If I had to pick one love language for my husband, it would definitely be physical touch. He loves the feel of my hands on the back of his neck, wants to sit oh-so-close on the couch, and practically sits up and pants if I offer to scratch his back.

Physical Mismatch

This is a challenge for me. I have never been much of a physical touch kind of girl. You see, I grew up with parents who loved me, but were not physically affectionate. My mom, who grew up in a strict German household, had to be taught how to hug. ("OK Mom, when I put my arms around you, that would be the time to put your arms around me...")

It just wasn't part of my makeup. But knowing that it was important to Roger, I knew that it had to become important to me, as well. Since getting married, I've studied books on massage, done some major damage in our local Bath & Body Shop, and made sure that touch has become an important part of our evening routine.

For most guys, touch is vital to relaxation. If this area isn't natural for you, I understand. Let me recommend an excellent book that has helped me: *Complete Massages: A Visual Guide to Over 100 Techniques* by Clare Maxwell-Hudson. Not only is this book easy enough for beginners, it's one of the only books on massage that doesn't result in shock, horror, and embarrassment should your mother-in-law come across it on a visit. The pictures are clear but mostly G-rated.

And yes, I do know what massage leads to. Just combine this with one of the Bonus Projects.

Is Your Husband a "Hands-Off" Kind of Guy?

So he's not into massage? That's okay. There are plenty of other ways to meet your guy's physical needs.

Is there something that bothers your husband physically? It could be the lumpy pillows on your bed, the lack of a comfy blanket on the couch, or a scritchy-scratchy tag in one of his dress shirts. Think about a way that you could add a little creature comfort to his day. Perform a tagectomy on that shirt, replace those pillows, or place a snuggly blanket within reach of his favorite spot in the living room.

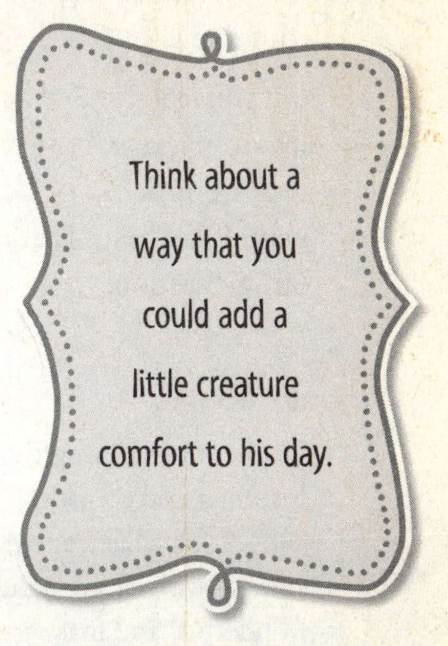

Even something as simple as building a fire to greet your husband on a rainy night could be a great way to give him some physical comfort after a long day.

Let's Get Physical

Take your cues from your guy. If you know he craves your touch, look for small ways to incorporate touching into your day. Perhaps a hand on his knee while he's driving, your arm casually around his waist while you're chatting with friends after church, or snuggling close while watching *CSI.*

Prayer for Today

Dear God, help me to step out of my comfort zone and love my husband in a way that meets his needs.

Getting Creative

- I'm way more inspired to do this project when I've just purchased a new lotion or massage oil. Run to the mall and buy a jar of "inspiration."
- Get some luxurious new sheets. Whether you're into silk, bamboo, or flannel, buy the best quality you can afford. Make your bed a cocoon that you can both snuggle down in and resist getting out of.

- People let their pillows go far too long without being replaced. Take a look at yours. Do they say luxury or limp, lumpy, and lifeless? May be time to lay your head on something new.
- Do you feel stymied because you know your husband would love a massage, but you have no idea how to do it? You can pick up a book, or better yet, ask him to show you what would feel best. There's nothing better than a little hands-on instruction.

Project Reports

"If there's one thing that'll bring my husband to his knees, accompanied by a long drawn out *ahhhhhh,* it's a hand massage. (Not what you were expecting, was it?) My husband loves it when I get some nice thick cream (Shea Butter is wonderful) and massage it into his hands and forearms. He's in heaven within about three seconds, and by the time I'm done, he's virtually putty. (And if you're wondering, this massage rarely leads to something else, because by the time I'm done he's already half asleep.)"—Teresa

"When we were dating I used to give my husband foot massages regularly. He kept saying 'When we get married this will all stop.' Not right after we were married but about a year down the road he was right—they became few and far between. Guess it's time to give him a nice long foot massage! I think I will add that into my weekly schedule."—Denise

"We've been sleeping on mismatched sheets for the past six months, so getting new sheets was not only what we needed, it was just in time for this project. Let me tell you how nice it was for the both of us to slip into Egyptian cotton bedsheets. Yeah, it was *nice.* You can get my point. OK. This one worked for the both of us."—Penny

"I love this. Not being a 'touch' sort of person myself, I realize this is an area I've (selfishly?) neglected. I happen to have just a little something tucked away from the last time I got inspired. Going to dust the bottle off, take a shower, invite my playmate to bed..."—Angie

"My husband has a lot of problems with his sinuses. So as we were relaxing, I had him rest his head in my lap and rubbed his head for him."—LJ

Your Plan for the Project *(copy your plan on The Husband Project Planner at the back of this book)*

Your Results *(his reaction, my reaction, etc.)*

Project 7

Trophy Wife

Looking Goooood for Your Man

Miranda Priestly: *"You have no sense of fashion."*
Andy Sachs: *"I think that depends on—"*
Miranda Priestly: *"No, no, that wasn't a question."*
The Devil Wears Prada

Your Project

Do one thing to look nice just for your guy. It can be clothing, hair, or makeup.

Most husbands are visual creatures. They love to be proud of the way you look. Is it possible, just maybe (please don't take offense here), that you're not putting in the effort you once did when it comes to looking your best? Do you get all dressed up to go out to dinner with your girlfriends, but put on the same old sweatshirt to grab food with your man?

I know, I know. Life is busy, you have a million things to do every day, and you don't need to look like a Barbie Doll every time you two run out to the grocery store.

The problem is, our men want to be proud of us. Doing our hair, putting on the cute jeans instead of the super-comfy (read: ugly) sweats, or even just putting on lip gloss shows that you care and are thinking about his needs as well. The next time the two of you are leaving the house together, take some extra effort in an area that you know is important to your guy.

This has been an especially tough challenge for me. I am not a "girlie-girl," but I'm not a tomboy, either. I just have never frequented the little boutiques looking for that one perfect pair of earrings that I knew would change my life. For some of my friends, their faces are a canvas, and Sephora, their paint supply store. For me, makeup is more of a necessary evil than an exquisite delight.

Comfort has always reigned supreme in my life, so the thought of putting my vertically challenged frame atop a pair of four-inch killer heels was about as foreign as walking on a pair of circus stilts.

That is, until I started dating Roger.

Suddenly I was spending a disproportionate amount of time and money at the Clinique counter. High heels (and a generous dose of Advil) were my constant companion. I knew he liked it when I dressed up, and I wanted to make him happy.

And then we got married.

Oh, I kept it up for a few months (a honeymoon fashion high). I wore cute jammies to bed, made sure my hair looked great when we went out for dinner, and painstakingly applied paints and powders to my face every day. But as Roger and I fell into a comfortable routine, I fell back into my comfortable clothes.

I'm focused on making sure I look the best I can with what God has given me.

So now I'm focused, once again, on making sure I look the best I can with what God has given me. I still wear sweats, but they're cute, flattering, and clean.

Recently, I went through my closet, giving Roger carte blanche over what I was going to keep and what I was going to donate. I'm now down to one tiny bar of clothes in my closet, but every piece of clothing in there shares two things:

1. It's something I feel great in
2. It's something that my husband thinks I look great in

This has given me a lot of freedom in clothing choices. I went from having racks and racks of clothes, but nothing to wear, to having a few pieces that I absolutely love. Getting dressed in the morning is much less of a chore and more of a delight.

If sweats are your unofficial uniform, like they are for so many women these days, make sure the central focus of your closet is not just your husband's castoffs. (If he's not wearing them, I'm sure he doesn't want to see you in them.)

This is not an edict to start running around in platform shoes if your main job in life is chasing after a toddler. This is an encouragement to be the best you can be, wherever God has put you in life. And please, make sure that at least some of your clothes are younger than your kids.

If You Are a Fashionista

Maybe you're one of those girls who grew up with a blush brush in one hand and a curling iron in the other. Looking good is not just a priority for you—it's a lifestyle.

Just be sure that you take into consideration your husband's likes and dislikes. I have one friend, Kristen, who had a passion for leopard-skin anything—shirts, jackets, earrings—plus had the personality to carry it off. She always looked elegant and appropriate, but at the same time someone you would ask to ride shotgun at a blowout bachelorette party.

When she got to this day of The Husband Project, she asked her husband about the leopard print. After he tried to skillfully avoid the question, the truth came out. Mark hated it.

"I could not believe it. Ten years, and he never told me." Kristen was crying as she explained the scene. "Ten years he has secretly hated how I looked."

I assured her that he didn't hate how she looked, maybe just a shirt or two. After the sting of rejection was over, Kristen decided to tone down the "Wild Kingdom" look. She realized she had gotten into a fashion rut as deep as some women who never get out of their black sweats, and she has started to explore some new options that are a little less jungle inspired. Plus, Mark seems to be noticing and giving out compliments a little more freely these days.

Finally, my last suggestion is to gear up, pray hard, and then ask your husband what he likes—and then listen to him. Have a couple of pieces of clothing in your closet, ready to wear, that you both enjoy.

Prayer for Today

Dear God, help me to see myself through my husband's eyes. Help me to be creative and have fun so that we can both find enjoyment in my appearance.

Getting Creative

- Take ten minutes and put three outfits together that you know you look hot in. If you don't own anything like that, then it may be time to take two hours and go shopping with a trusted friend to find some clothes that make you feel smokin'. Hang the pants, shirts, and accessories all together on the same hanger so that you have three cute looks ready to go the next time you're heading out for dinner.
- Every girl needs a pair of "go-to" jeans—those great ones that fit just right and look amazing with a pair of high heels or boots. Make sure your "go-to" jeans are clean and ready at a moment's notice.
- If this is an area you struggle in, it may be time to do some research. Do your homework by watching fashion TV (*What Not to Wear* or Tim Gunn's *Guide to Style*) or by reading up on the subject. One of my favorite books is *Simply Beautiful: Inside and Out* by Jill Swanson. Please note—I'm not saying you have to spend a lot of money. These days you can find cute clothes at Target and other less expensive stores. You just have to take the time to find the right fit and the right look just for *you.*

Project Reports

"My husband loves it when I get dressed up. I usually do, but last week I wasn't feeling well and really looked like something the cat dragged it. When I got back to fixing up, he noticed the change immediately. I have a pair of grey, well-fitted pants that he especially loves. When I wear them I usually get a little pat on the backside—from my hubby, of course!"—Becca

"A long time ago this preacher told me a story of a wife who, though busy, would always make an attempt to freshen up right before her husband came home and warmly greet him as he came in the door. Well, for my husband I try to do that daily. Sometimes I even go out to the car and plant a kiss on him that causes the neighbors to yell, 'Get a room!' at us once in a while. He enjoys that!"—LE

"I am so proud of myself. I have been looking especially grungy since I took the noon-parent job at school. One hour a day I look after 'my kiddos,' and I need to be comfortable and prepared for all kinds of weather since we're outside unless it's raining. My husband didn't say anything outright, but I decided I needed sweats that matched and even looked put-together in case I met him for a late lunch. I can't tell you the response since I hit Mervyns and Wal-Mart last week. My husband has noticed, complimented, and given me the old wolf whistle."—Angie

"Looking good has always been a desire of mine—a wonderful home ec teacher planted those ideas in my head. She said when you feel your worst, dress your best, and that has always stuck with me."—Pam

"Are you sure you aren't writing this just for me? I go in waves when it comes to this. Right now I am stuck in the down wave. I hate clothes shopping, and I really don't have too many preferences when it comes to clothes—well, comfy, but other than that none really, especially as I have gained some weight. I better ask my husband what outfits he likes best and then use my birthday money from our parents for a hot outfit!"—Sheri

Your Plan for the Project *(copy your plan on The Husband Project Planner at the back of this book)*

Your Results *(his reaction, my reaction, etc.)*

Bonus Project 1

Sex

Doing Your Homework

"Women need a reason for sex. Men just need a place."
BILLY CRYSTAL

Your Bonus Project

Pick up a book to do a little research into what your husband needs when it comes to sex.

It is time to talk about sex, ladies.

Your man needs and wants sex, possibly (probably) more than you do. If a man believes he is desirable to you, the love of his life, the other areas in which he may be struggling (work, parenting, golf game) seem somehow more manageable.

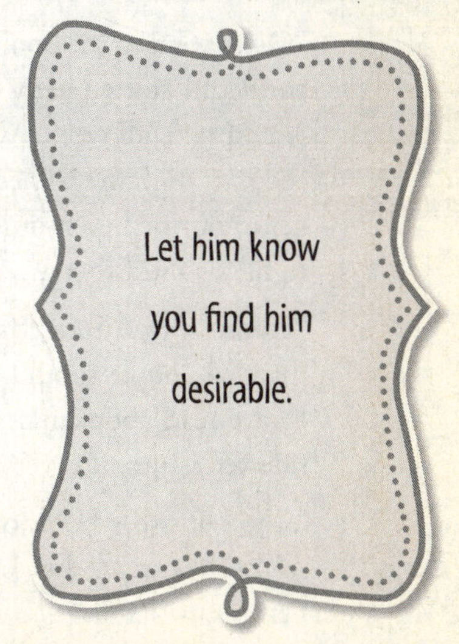

One time each week of The Husband Project, it is your job to initiate sex. For some of you, this is going to be way beyond your comfort zone. Do what you can. If it means snuggling, do that. The idea here is to take the first step and be open and tender.

Some of you may have a different issue. Perhaps your guy hasn't been all that interested lately—he may be stressed or struggling in other areas. The point is not to push it or make this another stressful event in life; just let him know you find him desirable. No pressure.

In my experience, it is better to shoot for earlier in the week to "make your move," so that if things come up (he has to work extra late, sick kids) you still have some time to check this off your list.

Prayer for Today

Dear God, I want my husband to feel loved in every area of his life. Help me to know how to love him better sexually, with Your guidance.

Getting Creative

In preparation for your romantic evening, I encourage you to pick up a book on the subject. Let it be your inspiration in case things have become a little predictable (or downright nonexistent). Two of my favorites, both by Dr. Kevin Leman, are *Sex Begins in the Kitchen* and *Sheet Music.* I also recommend Bill and Pam Farrel's *Red-Hot Monogamy.*

Project Reports

> "OK, I went to the bookstore, did some research, and he was thrilled! I started early on this project because I thought it would take all week. Well, it didn't. He was so happy that the next night he helped me put the kids to bed so we could get to our bed even quicker. He said to me, 'What did I do right?'"—Strawberry

> "I recently read *Sheet Music,* and it is an awesome book. Every married couple should read it. It's the first Christian book I have read about marriage and sex that is real and doesn't sidestep issues. It is very inspiring!"—Christina

> "Another great book on the subject is *Love Life for Every Married Couple* by Dr. Ed Wheat and Gloria Oakes Perkins."—Paula

"I did send a flirty text message, but I have to be careful since we just had a baby and are not yet allowed any 'boom boom' (as we've been calling it). So I will save the bonus date for a few weeks from now and try not to get anyone's motor running too terribly in the meantime."—MM

Your Plan for the Project *(copy your plan on The Husband Project Planner at the back of this book)*

Your Results *(his reaction, my reaction, etc.)*

Week Two Projects

Project 8

Location, Location, Location

A Special Treat in a Special Place

"It seems to me that our three basic needs, for food and security and love, are so mixed and mingled and entwined that we cannot straightly think of one without the others...there is a communion of more than our bodies when bread is broken and wine drunk."

M.F.K. Fisher, *The Art of Eating*

Your Project

Make it food and make the location fun. Really, that's all there is to this project.

It's food again, but this time it's all about setting.

In our culture, food is innately tied to celebration. If someone gets a promotion, has a birthday, or even scores an A on a test, the first words out of our mouths are often, "We should celebrate! Where do you want to go to eat?" I'm not saying it's the best plan (especially if like me, and half the other citizens of the United States, you or your husband struggle with weight issues), but it is a reality.

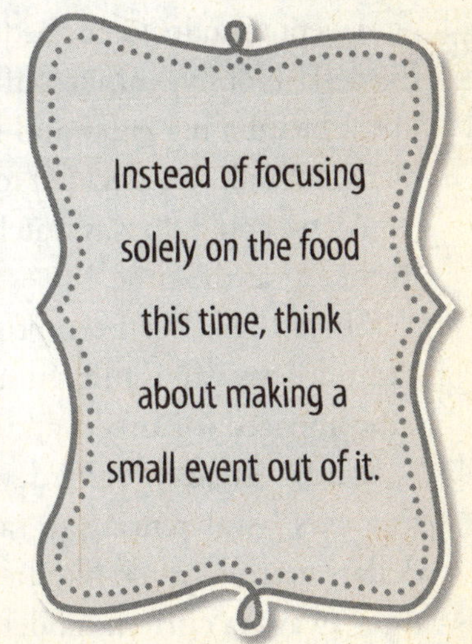

Many of my favorite memories with Roger are tied to food. When he proposed, he popped the question after grilling stuffed portobello mushrooms over an open flame. On one of our early dates, he took me to an amazing Mexican restaurant in the middle of winter, and we had tapas sitting next to a roaring fire. This past Christmas Eve, we had a carpet picnic eating pizza fondue and tangerines in the middle of our living room with our kids. While the food was important, the location is what made the experience memorable.

So, instead of focusing solely on the food this time, think about making a small event out of it.

A Different Kind of Drive-Thru

A tree ran into my car.

Yes, you read that sentence correctly.

I am blessed to live in Northern California where we bundle up in our winter woolens if there is a slight chill in the air, and the only snow we see is when someone forgets to use their Head and Shoulders shampoo.

So it was out of the ordinary when the storm rolled through town. Power outages were reported all over the city, fender benders littered the highways, and the Starbucks on our corner was closed.

Obviously, this was a desperate situation.

When I got home from my morning speaking engagement, I parked my van and ran inside, desperate to warm up and dry out.

I went upstairs to our bedroom, where my husband was working at his desk. Not five minutes after I got changed into dry clothes, Roger and I heard a big *crack* and looked out in horror and amazement as our giant oak tree decided to take up residence on top of my car.

All we could do was watch, laugh, and thank God that no one was in the car at the time.

Since then, I've been cruising around town in a series of rental cars until my van is fully functioning again. I've tried out hybrids and subcompacts, 4-runners and sedans.

Until yesterday. Yesterday, the rental agency ran out of the teeny-tiny cars I was renting to save money. They asked me if, for a few dollars more, I would like an upgrade to a nicer car that was available right away...a current model black Mercedes-Benz E-Class.

Um...OK.

I knew, being in possession of that car, I had to turn our ho-hum, stay-at-home night into an out-on-the-town date night. You wouldn't want an automobile like that going to waste, now would you?

Roger and I used a gift card to get a couple of lattes at a Starbucks drive-thru, and then took a drive into the mountains, sipping our drinks and enjoying the scenery and the company. A perfect date—all for the small price of an upgraded rental car.

There was just something so fun and adventurous about that car that it turned that silly little latte into a memory that will last us a lifetime.

A Cozy Corner at Home

A favorite spot at our house is the fire pit on our tiny back patio. In one of the top kitchen cabinets, hidden deep so that no one eats through our supply, is a stash of marshmallows, graham crackers, and Hershey's bars. While the s'mores are a family favorite, Roger and I also love to take coffee and hot cocoa out by the fire and sit and talk.

Location Plus Atmosphere

Think of some other ways to turn your treat into a memorable moment. I have an iTunes list of songs that I know are my guy's favorites. While I may never have thought to put together a list that includes Jars of Clay, James Taylor, and the soundtrack to *Shrek,* I know it makes him happy.

Maybe it's doing a tailgater at a football game, or going to his favorite coffee shop and reading the paper with him on a Saturday morning. Donuts in bed? Whatever would be fun for him is the Your Plan for the Project.

Prayer for Today

Dear God, teach me to create places of celebration—no matter how small—inside and outside my home that will make my husband feel loved.

Getting Creative

No need to get super fancy here. If he simply enjoys popcorn in front of the TV, that's OK. Some other ideas:

- If he enjoys being outside, how about dinner in the back yard? I have a friend who doesn't have patio furniture, so she actually drags her wooden breakfast table and chairs outside. It's not about resources, it's about creativity.
- One thing our family has done on several occasions, especially when the kids were little, was to do the carpet picnic. Spread out some quilts, watch a movie, and enjoy the great indoors. (This would be a good night not to serve soup.)
- Pack one of his favorite snacks for a long trip.
- For a more grownup encounter, how about a shower or bath with chocolates.

Project Reports

"I am going to shock the socks off my husband and get up when he does (4:30 in the morning), make him coffee, and bring him a cup while he is in the shower. He will definitely know something is up!"—SH

"Yummy yum! I made hubby's favorite Cheesy Chicken recipe. His favorite place for food is at the table with our family, so we kept the location traditional (have to go with what works for your hubby's personality/preferences). I might try for a picnic when the weather allows."—Karmyn

"Yes, it is all about location, location, location. Our favorite place is on the front porch. Whether it's a picnic lunch on paper plates or sit-down dinner (with the card table covered in a tablecloth and 'real' dishes), we have many great memories of eating/relaxing in our outdoor living room."—Sherry

"We were at my mom's on Thanksgiving break. I brought him breakfast in bed, along with the whole family. We all sat in bed for an hour eating our Fruit Loops, coffee, and bananas, watching cartoons. He loved it, said it was better than back in the day when it was just us."—Strawberry

"I'm going to set up a special lunch table in the staff room where he works. Food, candles, tablecloth, and cloth napkins. I hope he will react more favorably than he did to breakfast in bed."—Lynette

Your Plan for the Project *(copy your plan on The Husband Project Planner at the back of this book)*

Your Results *(his reaction, my reaction, etc.)*

Project 9

Hi-ho, Hi-ho

Working Together

"Coming together is a beginning; keeping together is progress; working together is success."
HENRY FORD

Your Project

Today, it's helping your husband to get the job done. Help him get one of his regular duties off his list, or come alongside him and assist in a project that he enjoys.

Does your husband know, beyond a shadow of a doubt, that you are in his corner?

My husband is world famous for his salsa (it's our own little world of friends and family, but still...). Whenever there's a BBQ, potluck, holiday celebration, or birthday, the one request is "Can Roger bring his salsa?" In fact, the day before our wedding, Roger and his two brothers and their wives spent the day slicing and dicing peppers, squishing tomatoes, and canning jars of salsa to give to our wedding guests as favors.

As you can see, round these parts, we take our salsa seriously.

I would never dream of asking Roger if he needed my help making the salsa (that would be akin to asking, "Hey Michelangelo, need any help with that ceiling?"), but I am more than happy being his sous-chef—shopping for ingredients, getting him the cutting board, cleaning up afterward.

I love being in the kitchen with him as he's chopping, dicing, mixing, and sampling his tomato concoction. It's a great time for us to connect, working side by side, enjoying each other's company, as well as being productive.

I know that during these times Roger feels loved and cherished, and he knows that I recognize his contribution to our household and lives.

Plus, he looks so hot in an apron.

Teaming Up

It could be as simple as taking out the garbage, cooking dinner, or washing his car alongside him. Offering to do a job *with* your man is a great way to get the job done and have some fun along the way.

I have always had the fantasy (I think along with most of my friends) that the way my husband and I are going to continue the honeymoon is by candlelit dinners and romantic strolls along tree-lined paths. A string quartet plays softly in the background, and builds to a swelling crescendo when he declares his everlasting love for me. That and the occasional large piece of jewelry will keep that loving feeling alive.

But the times I look back on with the most affection are the long hours we talked about love and life while reorganizing the camping equipment in the garage, or the time we tried to repeat a chicken picatta recipe that we enjoyed at a local restaurant. Not only is the work more fun, it's less of a chore when you work together.

Solomon got it right when he said, "Two are better than one because they have a good return for their labor. For if either of them falls, the one will lift up his companion. But woe to the one who falls when there is not another to lift him up" (Ecclesiastes 4:9-10).

The other benefit to working together is that you'll be able to complement and celebrate each other's natural strengths. Is there a part of a chore that your husband hates, but you don't mind or even enjoy? Support him in a loving and affirmative way by taking the part that you do well, and let his strengths shine. (Plus, if you're like Roger and me, you'll be happy to have your husband at the ready, able to reach the fire alarm when some of your cooking experiments have gotten out of hand.)

Charity Begins at Home

Another twist on this task is to work with your man on a project that's close to his heart. Is there a charity that you could give some time to, or perhaps a ministry that your husband is involved in that you could help out for a day? Letting him know that what is important to him is important to you will be a great encouragement to your husband.

Prayer for Today

Dear God, let my husband feel he has a partner in me. May he be blessed and supported by me every day.

Getting Creative

Make it fun and get his work done so you can both play.

- Does he enjoy cooking? Maybe he would appreciate a prep cook for the day. Let him perform his sauté magic while you chop, clean, and do whatever it is that will let him release the Rocco within.
- If he's one of those clean car freaks (we don't have any at our house, but I have heard they exist), use your HandyVac skills to clean the inside while he works on the outside.
- Would he rather work alone? Get him a cold drink or a hot chocolate to let him know you're grateful for all he does.

Project Reports

"My husband likes to do the dishes after dinner to relax. So tonight I will dry them while he washes. Should be fun!"—Strawberry

"This one is hard for us, since we have four kids; we usually have children helping as well. Also, I already take the trash out, wash the cars, and ride the mower. Yes, things I love that he does not enjoy. At times I feel like others look down on him because I do those things, but I am the one home and I have no problem doing them. Sometimes husbands just love it when we sit and watch them do something they love. For Jeff it's the Xbox. He loves it when I watch him play or attempt to learn and play myself. It's a stretch for me since I don't really like video games."—Sheri

Your Plan for the Project *(copy your plan on The Husband Project Planner at the back of this book)*

Your Results *(his reaction, my reaction, etc.)*

Project 10

Dress to Impress

Wear Something Just for Him

"I base my fashion taste on what doesn't itch."

GILDA RADNER

Your Project

Wear something just for him. You can go buy something or pick an item you already own. He doesn't need to know what you're doing—*you know, and that will change a little something inside of you.*

Not Just about the Clothes

There was a time in the not too distant past where I was ponytail crazy. Between hitting the gym, running kids to school and activities, and trying to produce an income to feed and shelter four teenagers, my hair was the last thing on my to-do list. It was enough work just getting to my stylist, Franc, once a month to guarantee that I remained a redhead.

The problem was, I knew that Roger hated my convenient hairstyle of choice. He said that he loved it when I wore my hair down, loose and curly.

That's when the inner monologue started. Perhaps you're familiar with this little speech:

> OK—fine, I get it. He likes my hair down (when I wear skirts, when I wear jeans instead of sweats, when I wear blue.) Doesn't he understand that it takes time to do all that "girly" stuff?

Oh sure, I could be perfectly done-up if I had a stylist and a makeup crew. All he has to do is throw on a pair of clean jeans and make sure there's no visible nose hair. Who does he think he is? Well, if he helped out more with stuff around the house, then maybe I would have time to look like I didn't just roll out of bed. I cannot believe how selfish he is!

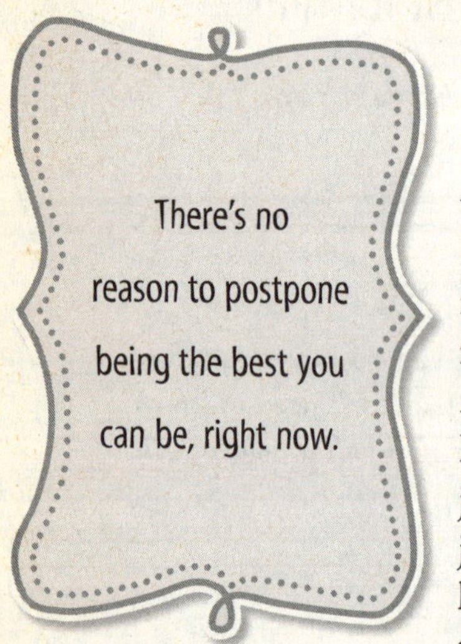

All this because he told me how pretty I looked with my hair down.

Poor guy.

Our husbands like being married to women. Not that we have to be dressed in Laura Ashley, looking like an extra from *Little House on the Prairie* in a flowered smocked dress. In fact, I get more compliments from my guy when I wear my leather jacket and favorite jeans than when I get all dolled up. He just loves when I make the effort to look like my full-time job is something other than ditchdigger.

Wearing my hair loose and curly, wearing his favorite color or the necklace he gave me last Christmas is just a little something to let him know that I'm thinking about him and care about his opinion.

Do a Little Research

Do you already know what your husband loves to see you in? If not, it may be time to do a little investigating, or even outright ask him.

The challenge here is that when you ask him, you also need to be prepared to listen to what he says. If he's brave enough to tell you that he's not a huge fan of the sweater with the feathers on it, then you need to respect him enough to stop wearing the sweater.

To ask and then ignore his opinion is much worse than never asking at all.

Beauty Without Vanity

Subconsciously, women may wrestle with wearing nice clothes or doing their hair and makeup because of feeling undeserving of such an *Extreme Makeover* wardrobe. Or perhaps it's a struggle because we might consider ourselves unspiritual or self-absorbed if we spend too much time on looking good.

I love how Jill Swanson, author of *Simply Beautiful: Inside and Out,* opens her book talking about "Beauty Without Vanity":

> Balancing beauty with humility is an ongoing struggle for today's woman. None of us want to appear vogue on the outside and vague on the inside. If we were to be honest with ourselves, we would all like to look the best we can. Clothing and appearance affect how we feel and think about ourselves. They can lift our spirits and help give us confidence to face the real world.
>
> The body is God's handiwork. We have a responsibility to take care of it and to present ourselves in a way that will compliment the Kingdom of God. How we appear on the outside reflects our integrity and competence. Through initial contact with people, fifty-five percent of our perceived credibility is based on appearance alone! First impressions lay the groundwork for establishing trust and believability.

Don't Wait Until "The Next 5 (or 50) Pounds"

Then there's the issue of putting off thinking about our appearance until we hit some mystical, magical goal.

- When I lose weight
- When the kids are in school
- When I go back to work
- When I get a better job

The problem is this: If you feel undeserving at 170 pounds, there is nothing magical about getting to 150 that's going to suddenly make you feel worthy of taking care of yourself. There is always someone thinner, taller, prettier, and who looks better in those jeans. There are millions of other women who, when you compare yourself to them, will leave you wanting.

The other side of this is that you're the only one of those millions of women who your husband is married to. He wants (and may I be so bold as to say deserves) the best version of you, right now, that's available.

I'm not saying don't lose the weight or give up on your exercise program. I've struggled with these areas all of my life, and they most likely will keep me on my knees in prayer until the day I die. What I am saying is that there's no reason to postpone being the best you can be, right now.

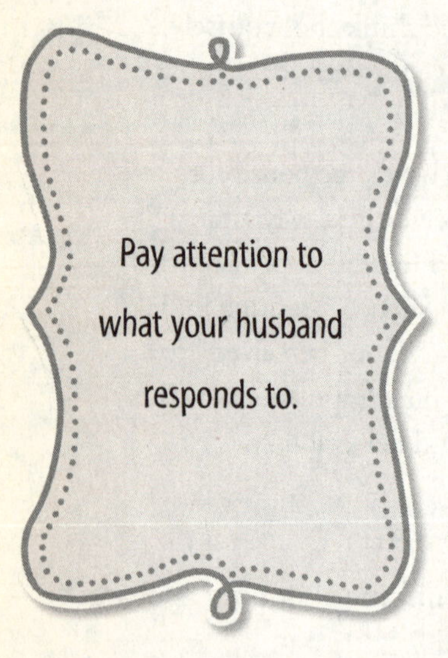

If money is an issue when it comes to clothes, you're better off having three outfits that you know your husband loves you in, and you feel great wearing, than a couple of closets filled with things that are comfortable but make you look tired and dowdy.

Pay attention to what your husband responds to. Does he give you extra attention when you're wearing a dress? Maybe it's time to commit to wearing skirts once a week. My husband gave me the most amazing turquoise pendant necklace for Christmas. I now have three shirt, jacket, and jean combos that look great with that necklace. And when I get a compliment, I get to say (loud enough for Roger to hear me), "I know, I love this necklace too. My husband picked it out. Doesn't he have great taste?"

Prayer for Today

Dear God, I pray my husband knows he's special to me in every way—that he is worth the extra effort.

Getting Creative

- Is your husband a sports fan? Maybe the sexiest thing you could wear is a T-shirt with his team's logo on it.
- The next time you're shopping, think about your husband's favorite color. Chances are it's blue—lucky us! Everyone looks great in some shade of blue. Make sure to mention that you bought it with him in mind.

Project Reports

"I bought a new shirt a few weeks ago. Every time I wear it he says, 'I like that shirt,' or 'That shirts looks nice.' So I wore that shirt today, and occasionally throughout the day I remembered his comments and felt more confident. He did not say anything this time, but he has said it enough before that I know how he feels."—Linda

"Today I will wear a pair of gold earrings my husband gave me. The card that he wrote when he gave them to me read 'I love you more each day.' So I call them my 'I love you more each day earrings.' (I'm not real creative!) He is impressed that I remember what he had written on the card."—Denise

Your Plan for the Project *(copy your plan on The Husband Project Planner at the back of this book)*

Your Results *(his reaction, my reaction, etc.)*

Project 11

Stress-Be-Gone

Eliminate Something that Makes Him Crazy

"Stress is the trash of modern life—we all generate it, but if you don't dispose of it properly, it will pile up and overtake your life."

DANZAE PACE

Your Project

Today's focus is to remove one stressor from his life. Figure out what makes him feel a tiny sense of defeat each day and plan to remove it.

My husband and I live in Silicon Valley where the dreams are big, but the houses are small. Our home measures in at less than 1300 square feet. With the two of us, plus three teens living at home and a cat with a weight issue, you've got the makings of some tight living quarters. Every square inch of our tiny townhouse serves at least a couple of purposes. The living room is also the kids' computer room. Our dining area is homework central, and our master bedroom is also my office.

I know Roger would love nothing more than to come home and be able to lie down for a few minutes at the end of a hectic workday. Unfortunately, his side of the bed is the only flat surface I can use for the layout space for my next article, "How to Organize Your Home from the Inside-Out."

One thing I can do to love Roger a little better is to make sure that the bed is clear of projects and folded underwear at the end of the day. One less obstacle between him and a few minutes rest will go a long way in giving him peace.

What in your husband's day makes him stifle a sigh? Does he have to remove a driveway-full of bikes before he can park his car? Is he a neat freak who comes home to *Mount Fold-Me* on the couch every day?

Maybe it's a carload of donations waiting to go to the Goodwill or a special screw he needs to pick up in order to fix the door. Whatever it is, see if there's a way to take the annoyance out of his life.

Wife Warning, Wife Warning

Here's a critical warning for this project—just because something is stressing you out doesn't necessarily mean it's stressing him out.

If you spend four hours organizing the junk drawer in the kitchen, getting it straightened to all of its obsessive-compulsive glory, and then you're crushed because your husband doesn't immediately swoon over your cleaning feat, perhaps he wasn't as bothered by the junk drawer as you were.

And maybe your expectations are a tiny bit unrealistic. Just a thought.

Prayer for Today

Dear God, let me do these things, not to be noticed, but so my husband will feel loved and honored, even in the little things.

Getting Creative

- Does the sound of Cartoon Network blaring when he gets home drive your guy nuts? Maybe some Mozart (or Credence Clearwater Revival) would be a better sound to greet him.

- Does your he-man need to wade through piles of makeup and "product" just to brush his teeth? Time to declare some man territory in the bathroom. Put your stuff in baskets or on shelves so he has clear access to all his gear.
- Where's his favorite spot in the house? If it's the chair by the TV, make sure the remote is handy (with some fresh batteries, perhaps) and his newsmagazine is close by.
- Are there a bunch of recordings your husband has been meaning to download on his iPod? Get your tech-savvy teenage neighbor to show you how to do that.
- Does he have a watch that needs a new battery, a piece of luggage with a broken handle that never quite makes it to the repair shop, or a favorite shirt with a button missing? Take care of the little annoyance, not to be thanked, but just to make his life a little easier and more hassle-free.

Project Reports

"One thing that really bugs my husband is my coffee cup collection. I just hate to get rid of anything, but they don't all fit in the cupboard. I guess I will just have to part with some of them today."—Denise

"One of my husband's annoyances is getting into the shower to find only a small, tiny soap remnant left on the shelf. His biggest contention is that I take up the entire shower caddy with my 10 different 'cucumber melon papaya mango coconut vanilla—there's a produce section in our shower' bath gels, so why do I need to use his bar of soap! I made sure a nice fresh bar of soap was readily available."—Karmyn

"I went through all of the pens on my husband's desk, pitching the ones that were out of ink and replacing them with ones that could actually write."—Tamara

"Our kitchen and family room is one big room with a counter in the middle. As counters have a tendency to do, it gets filled with papers, my son's figurines, glasses, art projects, etc. It drives my husband crazy. I know he likes walking in from work to a clear counter, so each afternoon before he arrives home I try to straighten up so when he walks in he feels a sense of peace."—Sue

"My husband is retired and it drives him crazy that I leave my delicate wash in the dryer when I go to work. He would happily do laundry while I am at work, but he doesn't want to ruin my delicate things. So I will make sure that the dryer is empty before I go to work."—Mary

"I am very good at getting the laundry done and folding it. However, moving the folded laundry out of the basket and into the drawers is my least favorite chore. My husband complains that he can never find his clean clothes, especially socks, as they are residing somewhere in the bottomless hole of the laundry basket, hiding between the children's T-shirts and my jeans. My husband stayed out late tonight, going to our daughter's preschool meeting. I made sure all the clothes are clean *and* put away, so he won't have to face the laundry abyss in the morning."—Sheesh

Your Plan for the Project *(copy your plan on The Husband Project Planner at the back of this book)*

Your Results *(his reaction, my reaction, etc.)*

Project 12

Gotcha!

Notice the Great Things He Does

"Do not let any unwholesome talk come out of your mouths, but only what is helpful for building others up according to their needs, that it may benefit those who listen."

EPHESIANS 4:29

Your Project

Tell your husband something about him that you think is simply great.

What Men Really Need

One of the big things I've learned in doing The Husband Project is that for us as wives, giving words of encouragement is one of the hardest projects we have. Sometimes we get cranky about our husbands not expressing their feelings. However, the feedback I get from projects that involve encouraging our husbands is that they're often the most awkward and difficult for us to do.

And isn't that just how love is?

In his book, *What Husbands Wish Their Wives Knew About Men,* author Patrick Morley shares some keen insight about what men need most:

> After his relationship with God and his family, what gets your husband out of bed in the morning?...What makes him happy?...How is he fulfilled?
>
> Besides a second cup of coffee, your husband longs for his

> life to count, to matter. At the core of every man boils an intense desire "to do," to master his world, to shape the course of events. Your husband is made for the task. Yet, not merely task for task's sake, but task with meaning.

Our husbands are desperate to know that they're making a difference in the world, even if it's only their family's world. They need to know that their work, their interactions, their leadership, and their love are making a difference to the people around them—and you are their number one resource for giving them that feedback.

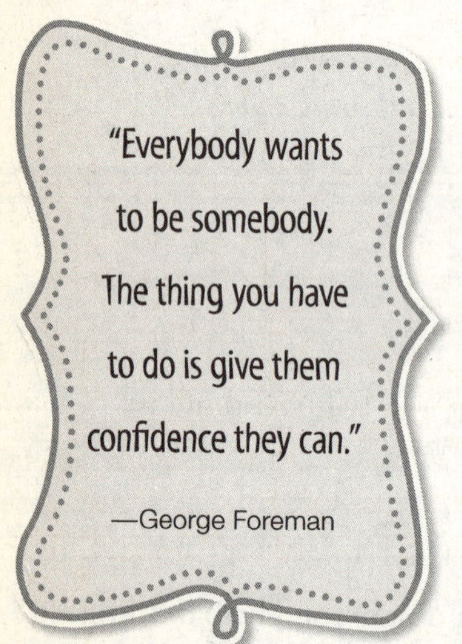

This is not natural for most of us. It's hard and uncomfortable to bolster our husbands with words—especially when we might feel, in our heart of hearts, that they don't deserve them.

But here's the thing. When you begin telling your husband how great he is, it raises his bar internally. Men, in every area of their lives, want to live up to the standard that has been set for them. He starts to see himself in a different light—not as the guy who is constantly missing the mark, but the one who surprises himself, and the people around him, with how capable he is.

Start Small

If this encouragement stuff is new for you, start small. Perhaps you grew up in a home where the only encouragement you received was when someone wanted something from you. That would naturally make you leery of handing out compliments too freely—it would seem disingenuous, maybe even fake. You would understandably be wary.

So try something tiny at first. Compliment you husband on something simple. Say he unloaded the dishwasher before you got home.

Make sure to notice and thank him for this small act. (OK, for some of you this would not be small. My friend Tina says this would be akin to her husband jumping up in the sink and walking on the dishwater.)

I can hear it now. "Why should I thank him for keeping the house going? It's part of his job too!" The same reason you would like to be thanked for picking up the dry cleaning or cleaning the toilet. Because it's nice to be appreciated. And we all need it.

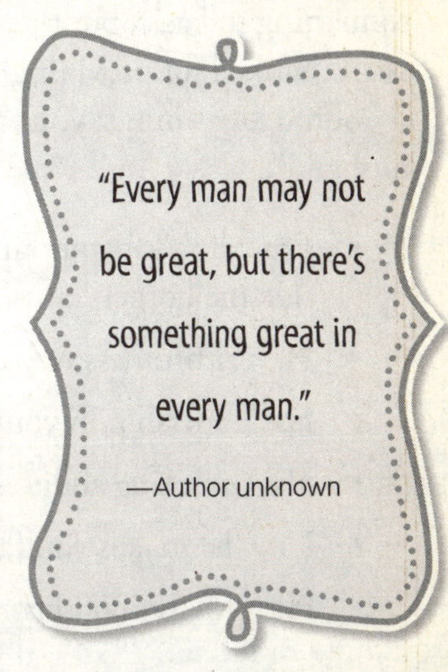

Plus, once you start to actively look for good things in your husband, you'll start to notice more and more of what he does.

Several years ago, I was looking to purchase a new car. Many people were saying great things about the Toyota Sienna. Because I had a relative who worked for Toyota, I bought the van without actually seeing one in person.

Once I drove my sand-colored Sienna off the lot, I was amazed at how many other sand-colored Siennas there were on the road. At school, at work, at the grocery store, and at church, *everywhere I went,* I saw sand-colored Siennas.

Had Toyota flooded the market with Siennas the day I drove off the lot? No, it just felt that way because now those vans were on my mental radar.

It's the same way when we're looking for ways to encourage our guys. If we aren't looking, we aren't seeing. But as soon as we look for ways to cheer him on, we're overwhelmed with ways to encourage him. As the Book of Proverbs puts it:

> He who seeks good finds goodwill,
> but evil comes to him who searches for it.
> (Proverbs 11:27)

Go Big

If you're an encourager by nature, or know that your husband is in real need of some atta-boys, it may be time to go big. When was the last time that you thanked your husband simply for going to work each day (or if he is out of work, for looking each day)? It seems like something so basic, but there are plenty of men who have never once been thanked for providing for their family.

Some big things you can focus on when encouraging your husband:

- Providing for your family (even if you're both working outside the home)
- His faithfulness to you
- His leadership in your home
- His parenting abilities
- How he makes you feel about yourself
- His provision of security in your home

Prayer for Today

Dear God, my husband has so many great qualities I can tend to overlook them. Let me see him with new eyes today.

Getting Creative

- Keep a 3×5 card in your pocket today. Every time some great quality about your guy comes to mind, make a note of it.
- If you're having a little trouble coming up with items for your list, ask around. Ask your friends, your mom, your kids—anyone who is a fan of your man can point out all the good stuff.

Project Reports

"This was a challenge to me today. I was not in the best of moods and feeling very irritable. Because of this project, I tried to put those feelings aside and focus on the things he does do. When he got himself a snack in the afternoon, I said, 'That looks good. I think I'll have some too.' Since the dog was lying with her head in my lap, he said he would get it for me. He does things like that all the time, and I do not acknowledge that he does these little things. When he came back into the room, I said, 'Thank you so much for that. You are always doing such sweet nice things for me.' His response was precious; he started to smile, but tried to restrain it and said, 'You're welcome.' He said other words, but I cannot remember them. Basically he was downplaying what he did, but was secretly thrilled for the praise. I need to work on praising him more for the things he does do. Thank you, Kathi, for this project in helping us see ourselves more clearly. It also made me not run off with my irritations and instead focus on him."—Linda

"I sent him an e-mail to let him know just how much I appreciate his hard work at providing the money. He works hard so I can stay home with the kids."—Strawberry

"My husband is so good at doing this for me, so it was a real treat to do it for him. I made a long list and presented it to him at dinner. I sat on his lap and read it out loud to him, and it made him smile. I think this project is very timely because it's been hard at his work lately."—Kirsten

"When I read this one this morning, I thought, *This will be easy...I love so many things about my husband, it will be an easy one to check off my list.* Little did I know that when he returned from work, we would have a discussion that turned into a pretty harsh revelation about something I need to work on in our marriage. *Ouch.* For a while, I went in the kitchen alone to make dinner and have a little pity party… and then I remembered my assignment. With a heavy heart, I approached him and put my arms around him and thanked him for the gift he is to my life and for the qualities I admire and respect in him that strengthen our marriage. I wouldn't have imagined how much I'd have to swallow my own pride to give him this blessing, but I'm so glad I did. Our evening ended with forgiveness and snuggling…and a renewed thankfulness in my heart for my husband."—Amanda

Your Plan for the Project *(copy your plan on The Husband Project Planner at the back of this book)*

Your Results *(his reaction, my reaction, etc.)*

Project 13

On My Mind

Turning Your Thoughts toward Him

"How lucky I am to have something that makes saying goodbye so hard."

ANNIE, FROM THE MOVIE BY THE SAME NAME

Your Project

Set up reminders during your day to think and pray for your husband. Let him know sometime during the day that he has been on your mind.

Thinking of Him, on Purpose

Your life is so busy that there are days when showering suddenly seems like an unaffordable luxury. Your to-do list makes you feel done-in (even though nothing ever seems to get *done*). Many of my days seem to be over before they really got started. I have grand plans of writing the great American novel, redecorating our bedroom, and cooking gourmet meals for my family. The reality? Most often it is writing an e-mail, making the bed, and mac-n-cheese. There are days when I could go for hours, so totally involved in the minutiae of my own existence, I can forget to really think about, or pray for, my husband.

Not that my husband is forgettable, by any stretch of the imagination. But he rarely needs a ride to Haley's house, doesn't have teenage dating drama, and is able to self-monitor his computer time, unlike the other members of our household. He's pretty self-sufficient, so it's easy for me to let him cruise on autopilot while I meet what seem to be more pressing work and family needs.

But my husband desperately needs my prayers. I know this—even though on many days, unless I'm intentional about praying for him, my whole day can slip by with nothing more than a nod toward heaven on Roger's behalf.

I can somehow find time to eat, read, and watch the occasional *Gilmore Girls'* rerun, but prayer seems a little out of reach.

That's why I must be sure to make prayer something other than a footnote in my day. Roger and I have made it a habit to pray for each other while he drives to work (who knew a key element to improving my prayer life would be Bluetooth technology?). It's at this point that I can learn what's pressuring him each day and how I can pray for him throughout his time at work. I also have a reminder on my Outlook calendar to lift him up throughout my days of working and carpooling.

What can you put in place to remind you to think about your husband throughout the day? Be creative. Maybe it's a picture of him on your dashboard or spraying his cologne on a scarf and keeping it in your purse. Whatever it is that reminds you of him, keep it around so you can call him later that day and say, "You've been on my mind all day." Trust me, it will make his day.

Calling to Share the Love—Not the Load

Once you've prayed for your man, it may be time to let him know he's been on your mind. I say *may,* because it depends on the reason for your call. If your call is to let your husband know that you love him and that you've been thinking about him throughout the day—pick up that phone.

However, if you're not totally intent on blessing him, think (and pray) before making that call. If you feel the need to vent, call your best friend or your mom—then call your man to let him know how great he is. I'm not saying hide things from your husband, but if you're having a lousy day and your husband is not in a position to help, why share?

On most days, our goal should be to infuse our man's day with love and light—not to burden him with our load. Obviously, if something big is going on in your life, and you need the love and support of your guy, there's no reason to hide things from him. You know your husband and what a phone call during the day means to him.

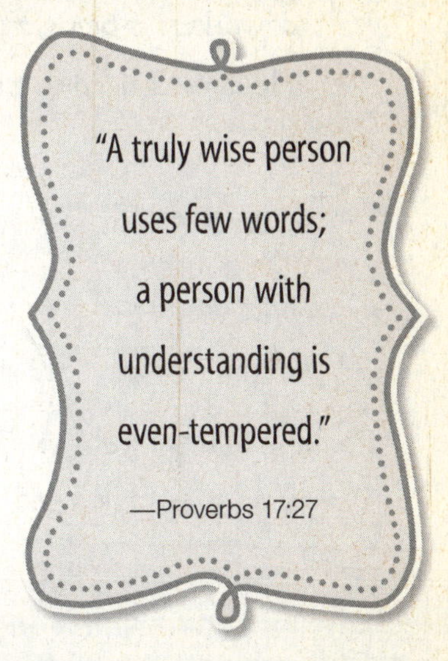

How would your husband react if, instead of calling him to vent or even rant about how the kids have finger painted the cat again, you called, not wanting anything but to tell him that you've missed him today.

Not Calling—Sometimes the Best Gift You Can Give

If you're one of those women who calls 12 times a day to let your husband know you ran out of low-fat mayo, perhaps the best gift you could give him would be not to call at all.

Part of the fun and excitement of dating is that sense of wonder, a tingly and eager anticipation. He thinks, *What is she doing right now? Is she thinking about me?* Once we get married, there tends to be an eventual lack of intriguing surprises. We know everything about each other. He knows what you look like in the morning pre-tooth brushing. He knows you at your best and at your worst. He knows all those little things that no one else knows. And that's the problem.

Give him a chance to *miss you.* Leave a little mystery in the relationship. If you wonder why he doesn't ask you about your day when you get home, perhaps it's because you've been sharing every detail, moment by moment, throughout the day.

Here are some good boundaries for phone calls:

- He doesn't need to know what you had for lunch, unless he asks.

- He doesn't need a detailed rundown of every awful thing your kids have done. (Does he tell you every time one of his coworkers is being a pain in the rear?)
- He doesn't need to know that you forgot something at the store.

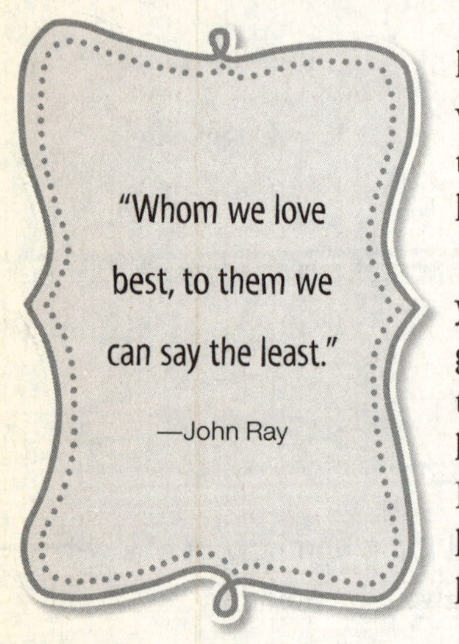

I know these sound crazy in the cold light of day, but these are actual conversations I've overheard, and they're the main reasons the wives called their husbands.

Make sure that you're attuned to your husband's natural rhythms. My guy is happy with a phone call during the day (in fact, he usually calls me at least once a day), but on his busiest days, I know it's better to just send an e-mail letting him know that I'm praying for him and thinking of him.

Prayer for Today

Dear God, let me speak when words are an encouragement.

Getting Creative

- Set an alarm on your cell phone for every couple of hours today. Let this be a reminder to stop and pray for your husband throughout the day.
- Do you have a picture of your husband on your cell phone? Make sure you do so that when he calls, his cute face will show up on your screen. (Ask a techie teenager to show you how to program this on your cell.)

Project Reports

"The best way for my husband to know I've been thinking about him during the day is to have his iced tea brewed and ready when he comes home. Another phone call interrupting his day does not communicate love for him. I just have to leave a sticky note reminder for myself to remember to brew his tea."—Karmyn

"I always check in with my husband because he leaves for work at 4:00 a.m. So I usually call him and say good afternoon around 7:00 a.m. Then I go into talk about questions for the day. Well, today I called him and sang our song to him over the phone. He laughed and thought it was really cute. He said thanks for the laugh."—Strawberry

"I decided to send e-cards to let him know I'm thinking of him. I signed up for a 30-day trial to Yahoo Greetings. I found a couple of laugh-out-loud funny ones that appealed to me. I plan on sending him a different e-card each day for the next week, starting today. If he likes it, I will keep the subscription. He's worth the $13.99 annual fee!"—sugga_lamb

"On the way home from the repair shop (where my husband followed me so I could pick up my car), I took a detour into a Starbucks coffee shop. He loves white chocolate mochas, and I was sure he hadn't had one in awhile. While I was waiting for the coffees, I called him and said, 'I'm no longer in front of you. I stopped in a Starbucks to get us coffees.' He said, 'Really? Can you get me a white chocolate mocha? I haven't had one in awhile and have been thinking of getting one.' I told him I already had, and I would be home very soon with it."—Linda

Your Plan for the Project *(copy your plan on The Husband Project Planner at the back of this book)*

Your Results *(his reaction, my reaction, etc.)*

Project 14

Move Over Rachael Ray

Cook Something for Your Husband

"If more of us valued food and cheer and song above hoarded gold, it would be a merrier world."

J. R. R. Tolkien

Your Project

Make your husband something special in the kitchen (reservations don't count).

It's an unfair fact of life—men like a woman who can cook.

Most of us didn't grow up with a mom who passed down an exceptional culinary legacy. Many of our mothers were out there bringing home the bacon *and* frying it up in a pan (or nuking it in the microwave before she had to get a bunch of kidlets off to soccer practice).

My mom worked outside the home and is a great cook. But, as with her sewing skills, natural cooking abilities skipped a generation.

In my first tiny apartment living alone, I survived for a year on take-out food and ham sandwiches. I was deathly afraid of cooking anything as complicated as chicken, fearing that I would certainly poison any partakers with a lethal case of salmonella.

When I got married, however, I quickly realized that my groom would not be quite so satisfied with a steady diet of take-out sushi, yogurt smoothies, and Diet Coke. It was time for me to spend some quality time with my soon-to-be new best friend, Betty Crocker, and learn to cook.

Diving into the culinary deep end, I tackled teriyaki chicken.

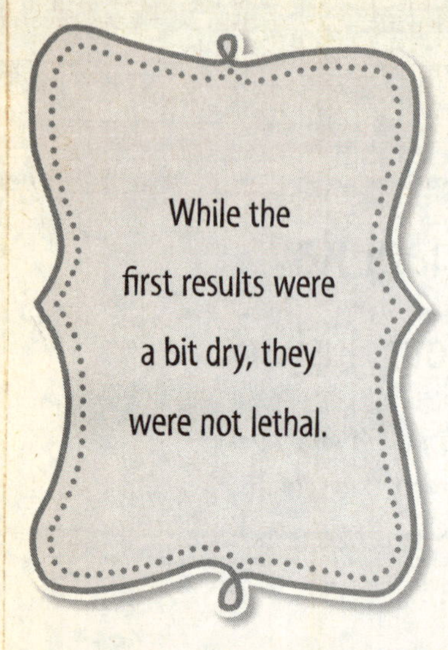

While the first results were a bit dry, they were not lethal. This gave me confidence to try and jump a few more epicurean hurdles.

If you're not a cook, but you know that your husband would like for you to be, here are a couple of fail-safe recipes that I know you can do, and that your husband will love. How can I be sure? Both our teenage boys cook and eat the following recipes. If they can cook them, you can cook them. If they will eat them, your husband will eat them.

Each of the recipes listed is great to prepare ahead of time for the freezer. However, you can skip freezing and put each dish straight in the oven if you are serving it the same night you assemble it.

Baked Ziti

1 pound ground beef
¼ cup chopped onion
16 ounces penne pasta, cooked and drained
6 cups canned spaghetti sauce
6 slices mozzarella cheese
½ cup Parmesan cheese

1. **Prepare:** Brown ground beef and onions together in a large skillet. Drain. Add spaghetti sauce. Combine meat-and-sauce mixture with cooked pasta; mix well.

2. **Freeze:** Spread pasta in 9x13 pan and cover with foil. Attach two freezer bags to pan, one with the mozzarella cheese slices, one with grated Parmesan cheese. Freeze.

3. **Serve:** Thaw casserole and cheeses. Remove foil and place mozzarella cheese slices over casserole. Sprinkle Parmesan cheese over casserole. Replace foil and bake at 350° F for 30

minutes, or until the cheese is bubbly. Remove the foil and bake for 5 more minutes.

Serves 4

Chicken Cacciatore

1 pound boneless, skinless chicken breasts
1 tablespoon vegetable oil
1¼ cup onion sliced
2 cups mushrooms sliced
1 teaspoon minced garlic
1 28-ounce can crushed tomatoes in puree
2 tablespoons dried parsley
¼ teaspoon pepper
2 teaspoons Italian Seasoning spice
1 teaspoon basil
¼ cup Parmesan cheese

1. **Prepare:** Cut chicken into cubes. Slice onions and mushrooms. Mince garlic.

2. **Cook:** In a large skillet, sauté chicken in vegetable oil until no longer pink in the center. Remove chicken from skillet and sauté onions, mushrooms, and garlic until the onions are transparent. Add chicken and remaining ingredients except for Parmesan cheese. Simmer for 15 minutes, stirring occasionally. Allow sauce to cool.

3. **Freeze:** Freeze in a 9x13 pan.

4. **Serve:** Thaw sauce in the refrigerator overnight. Place the foil-covered pan in a 350° F oven for 30 minutes to warm. Sprinkle with Parmesan cheese and serve over pasta or mashed potatoes.

Serves 4

Teriyaki Chicken

I make this marinade again and again. It is much better than any prepared marinade you can find in the store.

4 each chicken legs and thighs (or six chicken breasts)
½ cup soy sauce
3 tablespoons honey
1 teaspoon grated, fresh ginger
1 clove garlic, minced
2 green onions, thinly sliced

1. **Prepare:** Place the chicken in a gallon freezer bag. Mix the remaining ingredients together in a bowl. Pour the mixture over the chicken; fully coating each piece. Seal the bag.

2. **Freeze:** Place bag in another gallon bag and lay flat in the freezer.

3. **Serve:** Defrost the chicken. Pour off marinade and bake chicken in a pan at 350° F for 30-40 minutes (or until no longer pink in the center).

Serves 4

Need a little more inspiration? Check out this list of cookbooks for noncooks:

- *365 Ways to Cook Chicken: Simply the Best Chicken Recipes You'll Find Anywhere* by Cheryl Sedeker
- *Betty Crocker Cookbook: Everything You Need to Know to Cook Today*
- *Rachael Ray 30-Minute Get Real Meals: Eat Healthy Without Going to Extremes*
- *Desperation Dinners! Home-cooked meals for frantic families in 20 minutes flat* by Beverly Mills and Alicia Ross
- *The New Basics Cookbook* by Julee Rosso and Sheila Lukins (combines the information today's cooks need with irresistible recipes for the foods they want to prepare)

The Love Child of Emeril and Paula Deen

Yes, I realize that some of you can cook—quite well, in fact. So let me ask a different question. What are you cooking?

If your husband is mad about Sloppy Joes, but they offend your culinary senses, how does it benefit him that he married a great cook if you won't cook for him? It may be time to indulge one of his food fantasies and serve him what he wants—man food.

Man food is the stuff of great debate around our house. There is never enough salsa, chips, mini pizza, or chicken wings around here to satisfy the three men of the house. (I don't know how we could afford to keep a roof over our heads if I didn't limit the amount of guy food consumed by my two teen boys.)

I do realize that it's important to give a nod to this form of haute cuisine. Roger had been a single dad for thirteen years when we married, so to suddenly start eating grilled chicken and farmer's market salads three nights a week would put a strain on his delicate system.

So once or twice a week, I celebrate the men of the house by making chili cheese dogs, beef stew, or some other artery clogger with way too much salt. "Guy food in moderation" is my motto.

If guy food is a new concept for you, be sure to look at the list of recipes in "A Chick's Guide to Guy Food" in the back of this book. There you'll find several recipes that will put hair on your chest (or at least make your husband really, really happy).

Prayer for Today

Dear God, I pray that my husband knows my love for him by my efforts, not just the results.

Getting Creative

- Make one night a week your husband's favorite food night. Maybe Friday is the best night to do steaks or burgers on the grill.

- My husband loves it when I cook breakfast for dinner. Pancakes and sausage anyone?
- One of our most successful dinners ever consisted entirely of "bar food": buffalo chicken wings, potato skins, nachos, and quesadillas. Yum.

Project Reports

"Okay, this one is good for Jeff and me. I love really, really healthy dinners. Jeff loves steak and potatoes, steak and potatoes. I would be happy to have steak only once a month. And it would have to be an expensive one at that. I do find that Jeff brightens up and is more appreciative of my cooking and efforts when the meal falls in the category of foods he enjoys."—Sheri

Your Plan for the Project *(copy your plan on The Husband Project Planner at the back of this book)*

Your Results *(his reaction, my reaction, etc.)*

Bonus Project 2

Sex

Lingerie Shopping, a Gift for Both of You

"Nobody will ever win the Battle of the Sexes. There's just too much fraternizing with the enemy."
Henry Kissinger

Your Bonus Project

Buy a piece of lingerie that both you and your husband will love—then put it to good use.

Yep, we're going there. It's time to talk lingerie.

How's your lingerie wardrobe? A little outdated? Was the last teddy you bought something you got just before your wedding?

Oh, there's so much drama around this subject. Ever since Victoria let her Secret out, you cannot walk in a mall or watch live TV without having a push-up bra or lace thong thrust in your face.

And, even worse, in your husband's face.

How am I, a suburban housewife who has birthed two kids (both weighing in at almost ten pounds) supposed to compete with Gisele Bündchen in all of her airbrushed glory? I can't (duh), but that doesn't mean I should give up all together and resort to wearing footie pajamas to bed every night.

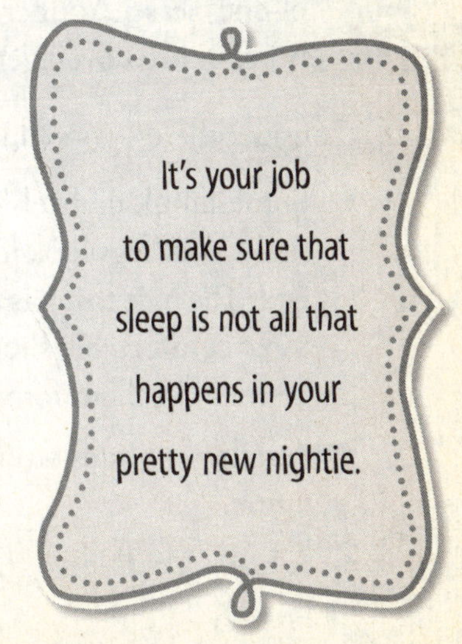

We've heard over and over that every woman needs a capsule wardrobe—select items of basic clothing that can be mixed and matched and updated with trendy pieces to get you dressed with confidence and out the door in a matter of minutes.

Now it's time to think about your capsule lingerie wardrobe—a few basic pieces in your favorite colors that all go together to make you feel fabulous.

Here are the basics that every woman needs to own and love:

- Silky pajamas—No, they don't show a lot of skin, but each piece can be worn separately (the bottoms with a silky camisole, the top all by itself). Plus, you have something cute and fun that keeps you covered when your in-laws come to visit.
- Silky camisole and boy shorts—These can be mixed and matched with the above items, or worn together when a more bare-bones approach is appropriate.
- A kimono—This style of robe looks great on everyone, and covers enough to run outside and get the paper while still looking cool and sexy.
- A lacy bra and matching underwear—Sure to be a crowd-of-one pleaser. Your choice on the style of underwear (thong, brief, or full coverage).

Consider these optional items to make things a little more fun:

- Some fabulous heels—Heels have the magical ability to make your legs look longer and give definition to your rear end. The nice thing is that it doesn't matter if they're not the most comfortable shoes in the world—you probably won't be wearing them for very long.
- A teddy—Hides tummy issues and looks great on every figure.
- A boa—I will leave that to your imagination.

Wear something sexy to sleep in. It doesn't need to be one of Victoria's sweet nothings—perhaps just a silky nightshirt or a lacy camisole. The goal is to dump the Nike T-shirt that you normally sport.

Also, it's your job to make sure that sleep is not all that happens in your pretty new nightie.

If you're feeling less than confident in the lingerie arena, check out Jill Swanson's article "The Real Woman's Guide to Lingerie Shopping" at the back of this book.

Make the extra effort to feel great about yourself. You know that some of that mood will rub off on your husband.

Prayer for Today

Dear God, sometimes I see sex as a burden instead of the gift it is for our marriage. Please help me feel confident in our sex life.

Project Reports

> "OK, this is too funny. The bottom drawer of my dresser has a big opening to the items inside. The bottom drawer just happens to be my 'silky nightie' drawer. Well, our two-year-old grabbed ahold of a cute polka dotted number (easy and quick access) and brought it to my husband. We both got a good giggle, and I received a very personal reminder for how to do my hubby project of the day."—Karmyn

> "I threw out an old T-shirt I loved to wear to bed—an old favorite with Troy Aikman on it. Aaahh. Anyhow, I took to heart some comments my husband had said to me and now go to bed with (gasp!) nothing on. I thought it would be an open invitation for sex all the time, but it hasn't been. But, boy, is he a happy man! He gets to look all he wants, and men are really visual beings. For his part, he got me an electric blanket that he turns on before I get into bed, which is so cozy. And, hey, I get to wear that beautiful robe I have. Everybody wins."—Annie

"I actually bought something special a couple of weeks ago, but it hadn't come out of the drawer yet. So I finally got it out last night and surprised my husband. He liked it, of course. Oh, I also wanted to comment that if you don't want to drop $60 on one of those 'sweet nothing' type things, I've found good stuff at Marshalls or TJ Maxx for very cheap."—Christina

"My husband travels, so when he is able to work from home, we enjoy having lunch together. The sweet little matching undergarments always add a little something to 'our dessert' time."—Elizabeth

Your Plan for the Project *(copy your plan on The Husband Project Planner at the back of this book)*

Your Results *(his reaction, my reaction, etc.)*

Week Three Projects

Project 15

What Not to Wear

Pitching the Pajama Pants

"Every time a woman leaves off something she looks better, but every time a man leaves off something he looks worse."

WILL ROGERS

Your Project

Get rid of one item of clothing you know your husband is not in love with. If it's a favorite that you'll have a hard time parting with, go ahead and purchase a replacement you know your guy will like.

We start off the week by getting rid of one piece of "comfortable" clothing. You know the one—it could be the pair of sweats, some comfy slippers, or a college sweatshirt. Your husband may not even notice that you've done away with it. The point is you're taking another step toward thinking about him when getting dressed instead of going to those sad, sad jammie bottoms once again.

Just get rid of it. That's all. You know what "it" is. For me, it was my pair of brown, cropped sweatpants that I thought were perfectly acceptable—but I knew that Roger secretly hated. I replaced them with a pair of cute brown sweatpants with a matching hoodie sweatshirt for when I'm working from home or running the kids to all their activities. This outfit is cute and comfortable.

A List of Ten Clothing Items that Should Never Be Worn Around Your Husband

Unless your husband has specifically said, "You look so adorable," while you're wearing one of these items, it needs to go. Don't make me come over and "What Not to Wear" you.

1. Team jerseys (unless they're your husband's team and you're wearing the jersey as a sexy nightshirt)
2. Overalls (unless you both work on a farm)
3. Running shoes for anything other than running
4. Mom jeans (super high-waisted, tapered, and pleated, oh my...)
5. Any sweater with a Christmas tree or a pumpkin on it. (Unless you're a kindergarten teacher. Even then, change into something flattering right after work. There is nothing sexy about wearing ornaments.)
6. Long floral dresses that tie in the back. They make your figure look dumpy and make you look like you're wearing a tablecloth.
7. Acid-washed anything. Enough said.
8. Underwear that has any form of safety pin attached to it.
9. Nursing bras. Especially if your child is now six.
10. Anything that an ex-boyfriend has ever given you.

When I e-mailed my friend Rachelle that I was working on this list, I got this note back from her: "Be *sure* to include baggy sweats on your list. When I figured that one out and traded all my baggy sweats for cute jeans and Ts and sexy leggings, well, let's just say things got a lot hotter around my house."

I rest my case.

Going Where No Man Has Gone Before

Have you taken a peek inside your underwear drawer lately? I don't care if you are a cotton briefs or silk thong kind of girl. The important thing is you don't take the attitude, "Who cares? Nobody is going to see it." Uh—hello. He does. At least if you're doing the bonus projects.

Our mothers had it right. If you were in a car accident and would be embarrassed by what you're wearing, switch it up. Pitch those worn, tired undies with the elastic coming apart and that used to be an entirely different color until they accidentally got mixed up with your husband's football T-shirt and now they're a shade of green not found anywhere in nature.

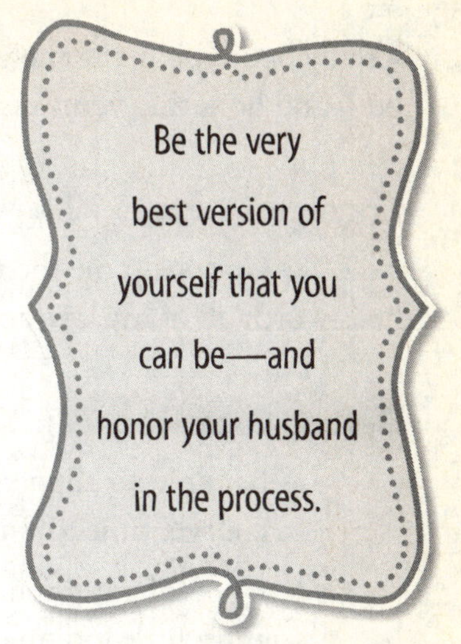

Tricks of the Trade

Maybe you have some great clothes but not the right tools to pull them off.

Several years ago I went to a stylist who helped me put some outfits together. I was amazed at the bag of tricks she had at her disposal to make my outfits go from pleasant to polished and put together. Here are a couple of items you may want to investigate before you throw out that great silk shirt that just doesn't look right or the pair of amazing black pants that are just a little too snug:

Spanx. These are better than a month on the cabbage soup diet. Spanx are "comfortable, slimming undergarments that flatter your figure." I don't know how they do it, but they work.

Shoulder pads. Don't worry; I'm not talking about the Joan Crawford/*Dynasty* kind of shoulder pads. I'm talking about the small, demure, almost-invisible kind that will give shape to too-narrow shoulders.

Hollywood tape. This is a wonderful invention. It's double-sided tape that can turn your favorite silk blouse that is just a little too revealing into something you could proudly wear around your grandmother.

Remember, this isn't about you giving up on your personal style;

it's all about you being the very best version of yourself that you can be—and honoring your husband in the process.

Prayer for Today

Dear God, help me focus on ways to let my husband know that he is worth all of my love and attention.

Getting Creative

- What do your slippers look like? If they're the pair you had in college, time to walk them out the door.
- For one of my friends, it was a hair scrunchie that was seeing a little too much time outside the house. (There was a bonus here because a number of her friends were about to have a scrunchie intervention. This project kept her out of a scrunchie 12-step program.)
- That sumptuous terrycloth bathrobe you got at the spa several years back has lost its "wrap me in luxury" feel and probably qualifies for pet bedding material. Time to find another robe, and the only strings hanging will be the belt ties.

Project Reports

"I've gotten rid of all the comfy sweats and now have nothing cute to wear. So I dropped a little hint for my husband about this great website he should check out for Valentine's Day. It's Pajamagram.com. It's a win-win situation. He gets to pick out something he would love to see me in, and I get a gift. I think he loved the idea!"—MV

"I had my own intervention today. I went through all my sweats and put the ones that were more comfortable than cute in the Goodwill bag. Just because they didn't look cute on me doesn't mean that someone else won't look cute in them."—Marie

"What a fun project! I went to the outlets where I found two huge stores of lingerie at great prices. I bought an elegant white nightgown and a flirty, fun, floral hot pink set... so *not* me! (I normally wear my running clothes to bed—pathetic, I know, but very practical). Hubby is traveling this week, but I'm looking forward to his reaction upon his return."—Karmyn

Your Plan for the Project *(copy your plan on The Husband Project Planner at the back of this book)*

Your Results *(his reaction, my reaction, etc.)*

Project 16

Is It Getting Hot in Here—Or Is It You?

Let Him Know You Think He's Hot

"I can live for two months on a good compliment."

MARK TWAIN

Your Project

In some small way today, let your husband know that you're attracted to him physically.

One of the things your man is looking for is affirmation. If he knows that you find him desirable and attractive, it goes a long way in giving him confidence in other areas of his life.

What drew you to him in the first place? I know he had a great sense of humor and was kind, but let's go shallower than that. What physical attribute did you first notice about him? Was it his piercing green eyes, his crooked little smile, his cute tush? This is the project to remind him that he still "does it" for you.

I Know—It's Not Fair

Most guys, as they get older, just get better looking. As grown-up girls, most of us like a guy with a wisp of grey hair and some laugh lines around the eyes. It shows that he has some character and experience in life.

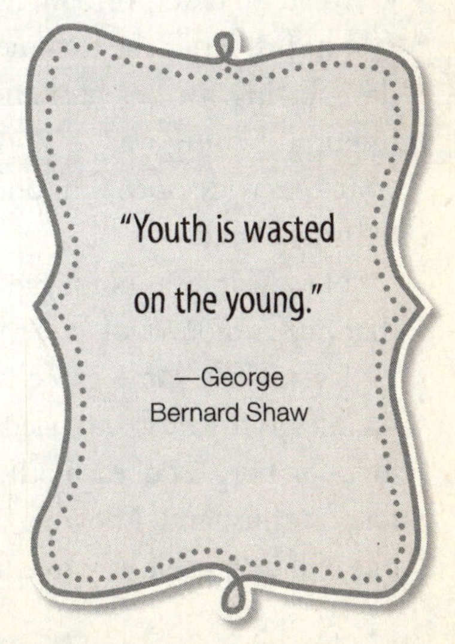

But when we think about women getting older, there are no words to describe the graceful aging process. (If anyone ever dares call me a "handsome woman," those may be the last coherent words to come from that person's mouth.)

If you call a man mature, you get the image of Sean Connery. A mature woman is more likely to remind you of your tenth-grade typing teacher who wore her glasses on a chain around her neck and had corrective shoes in brown, black, and navy.

So, while guys have a definite advantage in this area, we've found ways to level the playing field. We get to wear makeup, Spanx, and have facials and get our hair highlighted without our friends busting our chops. We have active ways to fight the aging process, whereas most guys are left with one option—to gracefully accept what time is bringing about.

It's that "gracefully" part that we can help with. While hubby may be losing some hair up top and growing it out his ears (can I just say right here and now, "Thank you, Jesus, that we women don't have to deal with *that*"), as long as he knows that you find him attractive, it will be a lot easier for him to accept getting older.

Rose Colored Glasses Are Required

I had an older woman, Mary, give me the best marital advice I've ever heard. After she told me that she would spend a bit of time each day praying for her husband and their relationship, the next most important thing was this: "You need to go into your marriage with your eyes wide open, but once you're in the marriage, keep your eyes halfway closed."

Now Mary was not suggesting letting sin go unaddressed, but rather that huge amounts of grace are required to make a marriage work.

I want the same grace when it comes to my not-so-lovely love handles as my husband needs with his growing forehead. We need to focus on the best of each other, in every area of our relationship—and for your husband, knowing that you still are in love with the shallow bits will be a great way to encourage him.

Show Him Your (Candied) Heart

If this is a new concept for you, it may be difficult to be fun and flirty—especially if the last time you told him how great he looked was on your wedding day. Why not flirt with some candy hearts? NECCO has been making these since the Civil War, and there is sure to be a heart to say exactly what's on your mind. Some of the original sayings still used today include:

- "Be Mine"
- "Be Good"
- "Be True"
- "My Man"
- "Kiss Me"
- "Sweet Talk"

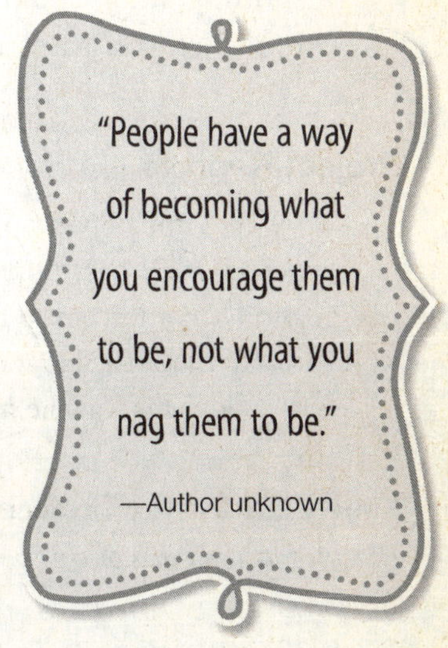

If none of those say exactly what you want, you don't have the option of ordering specialized hearts. (Well, you do, but the bad news is that the minimum order is 1.7 million hearts. The good news? They stay fresh for five years.) However, if you'd like an online version that you can customize, go to www.cryptogram.com and let your heart say what it wants.

Prayer for Today

Dear God, may my husband know that I am attracted to him and choose him above all other guys.

Getting Creative

- Looking for inspiration? Check out the Song of Solomon in the Old Testament. Talk about knowing how to show your adoration—woo-hoo.
- A little out of practice when it comes to flirting? Imagine

what you would love to hear from your husband and turn it around on him.

- Peek in on him while he's in the shower and just stand there. When he asks what you're looking at, simply sigh and say, "Just enjoying the show."
- No fair using your womanly wiles on him when he's performing a household task. The words, "Wow, you look so hot when you are scrubbing the toilet," are not allowed.

Project Reports

"Well, I am a little too private to tell you exactly what happened, but I communicated to my husband that he is sexy and I am attracted to him. The reaction I got was fantastic to say the least. He looked so surprised and so so so so so pleased. This was the number one winner so far."—Elaine

Your Plan for the Project *(copy your plan on The Husband Project Planner at the back of this book)*

Your Results *(his reaction, my reaction, etc.)*

Project 17

Playing Hooky

Give Your Guy the Night (or Morning) Off

"The mark of a successful man is one that has spent an entire day on the bank of a river without feeling guilty about it."

Author unknown

Your Project

Give your husband some time off. Hire someone to do his chores around the house (or do them yourself if money is tight). Just give him a chance to relax.

Men have a lot of responsibility in life. Not only is much of your husband's identity wrapped up in providing for you and being the man you need him to be, he constantly has to prove to the world his worth as a man.

Plus, the garage needs to be cleaned out.

On the oh-too-true-to-life show *Everybody Loves Raymond,* there was a wonderful episode where Amy, Ray's sister-in-law, won't stop talking to him during a basketball game on TV. When Ray mentions how much it bothers him, Amy replies, "I should've realized you're just a guy, and guys just want to relax and watch TV, and I should've left you alone." At this point, Ray's father, Frank, pipes in, "Amy, will you marry me?"

It's true—guys desperately want some time to just be guys and enjoy themselves.

How about giving your guy the night (or morning) off? If your husband normally spends Saturday morning mowing the lawn or doing other household chores, give him a get-out-of-chores-free card. Hire a neighborhood kid to trim the hedges or clean out the gutters. Let him know that *you know* he deserves a break.

Many of you are saying, "I would love to give him a break—if he actually *did* any chores." Hire the kid anyway. Your husband gets to relax, and you get to pull that chore from the "Honey-Do" (i.e. nag) list for a week.

"Pay careful attention to your own work, for then you will get the satisfaction of a job well done, and you won't need to compare yourself to anyone else. For we are each responsible for our own conduct."

—Galatians 6:4-5 NLT

I know that the area of household responsibilities is a hot-button topic in most marriages. For Roger and me, it ranks a close second to kid issues (and in a blended family, that's saying a lot). Many times we expect our husbands to have the same cleanliness standards that we do. We expect that because *someone* sees a pile of hockey equipment dumped in the entryway, *someone* should recognize that it's a fire hazard and people could fall and break their necks, and that *somebody* should do something about it.

The truth is that most guys are just not wired that way. So we whine and we nag and we "remind" our husbands. And still the towels remain on the floor, the dishes stay in the sink, and we stay teetering on the edge of madness.

Had much luck with the nagging?

No other human being is going to do everything we want, when we want, how we want. It just doesn't work that way.

I know, I know, your friend Laura's husband sends her flowers at work and does the laundry without being asked (and knows how to separate, fluff, and fold). It would be easy to look at their marriage and compare her husband to yours. But what you don't know is the struggle they have behind closed doors. We only get to glimpse what's happening on the front porch.

Every marriage is made up of a series of compromises, agreements, and grace. That's why it's important to understand and even celebrate those differences. As Leo Tolstoy once said, "What counts in making a happy marriage is not so much how compatible you are, but how you deal with incompatibility."

Whining and nagging get us nowhere. Being a counterculture, Christ-following wife may not change your husband's ability to see the crayon writing on the wall, but it will soften your heart toward him.

On the Other Hand

Some husbands might take offense to having someone hired to do one of their chores. This could be especially true if your husband struggles at work, is unemployed, or in some other way is feeling discouraged about his abilities. In no way do you want to give off the impression that you think he's not doing the job the way you want it performed, or even hint at the possibility that you figure the kid down the block could do it better.

If this is the case in your home, how about buying a tool to help him with one of his regular duties? A bag of chamois for cleaning his car, a rake to replace the one you bought when you first moved into your house, or getting a tune-up for his lawnmower are all ways to say *I love you* without making him feel like you don't think he's holding up his end of the bargain.

Remember, this is all about your attitude. It should never be our intention to "prove our point." The only point to prove is that we love our guy and want to show him our appreciation.

Prayer for Today

Dear God, I pray that my husband finds places of rest in his day. Let me contribute to that today.

Getting Creative

- Take his car to the carwash for him. Stock his ashtray with a Starbucks gift card to make his mornings a little brighter.
- Both my husband and I absolutely hate calling repairmen. However, if I make the arrangements, he's more than happy to deal with the repairman once the guy gets here. Suddenly, my part seems very manageable, and I feel that I'm letting my husband do what he is best at, while contributing what I can to the situation.

Project Reports

"I always find the time for my husband to have time to himself. He has a very stressful job as an air traffic controller, so personal time for him is one of my priorities. We set an amount of time daily for him to relax, and it pays off for the both of us."—Danielle

"As of two weeks ago, Saturday mornings are my husband's 'House All to Himself' time. I take everyone out of the house every Saturday morning around 7:45 a.m. until at least 10:15 a.m. Before we leave I set his coffee to brew at about 9:30 a.m. Hubby loves to sleep in and wake up to peace, quiet, and freshly brewed coffee! What a difference it makes for our entire weekend just by giving him some time Saturday a.m."—Karmyn

"My husband is not really good at taking personal time, but when the opportunity presented itself for him to go to a computer conference with his friends (just for fun, not work related), I actually encouraged him to go. He took the day off work and didn't get home until 11:00 p.m. He was giddy when he got home. He'd had fun eating out all day, catching up with friends, and doing something that would have bored me to tears. He loved it and was totally reenergized."—Laura

Your Plan for the Project *(copy your plan on The Husband Project Planner at the back of this book)*

Your Results *(his reaction, my reaction, etc.)*

Project 18

Dinner's on Me

Take Him Out for His Favorite Meal

Elaine: *"You ever notice how happy people are when they finally get a table? They feel so special because they've been chosen. It's enough to make you sick!"*

Jerry: *"Boy. You are really hungry."*

Seinfeld, THE CHINESE RESTAURANT EPISODE

Your Project

Take him out to his favorite restaurant.

I know why *you* like to eat in restaurants. Coming up with a plan to feed the two of you (made even more complex if you're feeding additional, and sometimes picky, members of the family) is only half of the struggle of fixing dinner. Then you have to shop for it, cook it, and possibly, occasionally, not even get thanked for it. A trip to the Olive Garden would be so much easier.

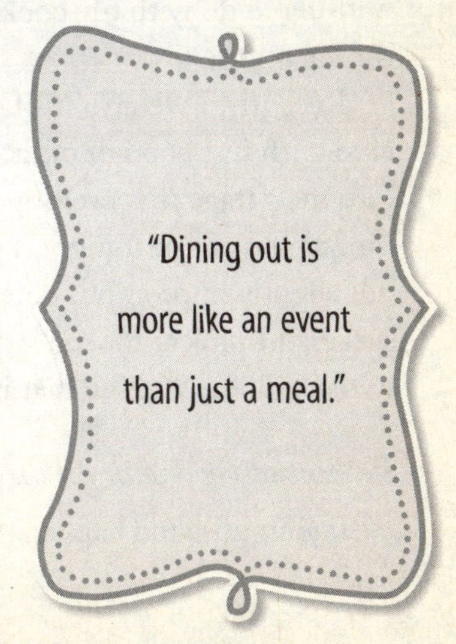

But why does your husband like to go out to eat so much? I asked a couple of friends to talk with their husbands about the appeal of eating dinner in someone else's kitchen. Here's what they had to say:

"My husband's response was 'a break in the routine' or, depending on the restaurant, to romance me. My thought was 'to get out of doing the dishes!'"—Sherry

"My husband said, 'Because it's relaxing, we get to focus on each other, and it's a special time.' I asked if it had anything to do with being able to get meals that he doesn't get at home. He said *no.* It has to do with being with me. 'We could go out to McDonald's and have a good time, I don't care.'"—Angela

"My husband travels frequently, so he eats many meals in restaurants. Despite that, we still dine out without the kids a couple of times a month. He says the appeal for him is to escape from our crazy schedule and have some quiet time together. More often than not, we combine dinner out with a movie, so in his mind, it's a good date-night event. He noted that since we also enjoy the art of food and savoring spectacular meals, dining out and sharing meals and desserts (which are usually not eaten at our house outside of holidays or dinner parties) is more like an event than just a meal."—Teresa

A Night on the Town—Ambush-Style

My husband loves to go out to dinner. He promises me it has nothing to do with my cooking; he just likes the whole experience of dining on the town.

Recently, I went to his favorite Mexican restaurant and got a gift card with just enough on it to cover dinner for two. When he drove into the garage that evening, I ambushed him and let him know that dinner was on me tonight. I jumped in the car, and we headed out on our slightly impromptu date night. That has probably been the most successful project for me so far; he still talks about how great it was to come home and see that it was all planned out.

Restaurant Food with All the Comforts of Home

If your husband happens to be one of those guys who really doesn't want to go out to dinner, how about bringing the restaurant experience home? Several of our favorite chain restaurants (Chili's, Outback Steakhouse, Applebee's) have online menus to order from as well as drive-up to-go windows so that you can zip in and out in the amount of time it takes them to ask, "You want fries with that?"

The Budget Night In

Is your man a huge fan of Red Lobster's Parrot Bay Coconut Shrimp or Outback Steakhouse's Aussie Fries, but has gone without because you're trying to stick to a budget?

I've discovered a great place to find those favorite restaurant recipes that you can re-create at home. Go to www.copycat.cdkitchen.com to find all those recipes that make eating out such a treat. With a little patience (and a lot less money) you'll be able to have your man's favorites waiting for him as he walks through the front door. And no credit card aftertaste to regret your choice at the end of the month.

Prayer for Today

Dear God, it's my deepest desire that my husband knows he is loved and cherished. Let my words, planning, and actions reflect that every day.

Getting Creative

- If you don't know whether your husband will be in the kind of mood that an ambush dinner requires, present him with the gift card to be used that night or on the night of his choice.
- Steaks on the BBQ when he gets home may be just the thing your man would love. See if you can duplicate the steak rub used at your favorite restaurant.

Project Reports

"It's easy—I just have Chinese ready for him. He'll love it!"—Stephanie

"We don't seem to be able to squeeze in the ambush meal these days, so on a Thursday at noon, right before he was getting ready to go out of town, I made his favorite lunch and lit candles and placed an orchid on the table. He looked at the table, smiled with a twinkle in his eye, and said, 'What is this for?' He was totally surprised and very pleased."—Elaine

Your Plan for the Project *(copy your plan on The Husband Project Planner at the back of this book)*

Your Results *(his reaction, my reaction, etc.)*

Project 19

The Service Here Is Excellent

Bringing Home the B&B Experience

"It is impossible to overdo luxury."
French Proverb

Your Project

Give your home the bed-and-breakfast touch by doing something a little extra special that both you and your husband will enjoy.

One of our favorite getaway spots is a little bed-and-breakfast in the mountains. If you ask my husband why he likes it so much, you very well might hear about the cheese and cracker plate with fruit that is always waiting for us when we arrive. (My thought has always been, *Great, we just spent the equivalent of a month's worth of groceries on a cheese and cracker plate.*)

Why We Love a Good Bed-and-Breakfast

What is it about the bed-and-breakfast experience that makes us want to fork over upwards of $200 a night to sleep on somebody else's sheets and eat clotted eggs in the morning?

- *Not being at home.* Nobody knows the phone number of the bed-and-breakfast, so as long as you turn off your cell phone, you're incommunicado. Your daughter can't hit you up for a ride to Susie's house.
- *The room is cleaned every day.* Now I know some of you

actually do this, but it doesn't matter. It's so much better and it just feels cleaner when somebody else does it for you.

- *The bed is made.* Now I know I'm spoiled, because my husband makes the bed every day. But how great is it when you're gone even for just half an hour, and you come back and the bed is done up. The pillows are fluffed and there's a little mint sitting there waiting to be indulged in.
- *Raid the pantry privileges.* This is the best invention of the modern hotel system since blackout curtains. I love the idea of going downstairs and rooting through somebody else's refrigerator. How great is that? And they don't have regular stuff like we have in our refrigerator; it's not just odd leftovers from a Christmas gift basket circa 1998 and some Gulden's mustard. There is actual food in the refrigerator. Food that my kids have not plowed through. I don't have to write my name on the food claiming that it's mine and touch it only under penalty of severe groundings. At the last bed-and-breakfast where we stayed, the pantry included all the fixings for mile-high sandwiches, a fruit plate, truffles, and chocolate-dipped strawberries.
- *Breakfast is served.* There's a just-cooked breakfast waiting for us when we get downstairs. (At one darling tree-house B&B, the owners actually brought the breakfast to us.) Nothing on the menu has been produced from a cereal box.
- *The bathroom counters are always clear.* Enough said.

Back Home and Back to Reality

Sadly, most of us can't afford to camp out indefinitely in the local bed-and-breakfast. So it's probably time to bring some of that bed-and-breakfast experience home. Here are a few simple tips from designer and author Kathryn Bechen (www.kathrynbechenink.com) to help you get that restful and relaxed feeling in your own bedroom:

- *Clutter Cutter.* Declutter your bedroom when you begin your fluff-up. Nothing kills romance faster than a pile of dusty magazines and techno paraphernalia.
- *Maid Brigade.* Next are the dust rag and vacuum. Turn on some music and make it fun!
- *Sensuous Sheets.* Purchase some colorful new sheets in a pattern you love with a thread count of at least 300.
- *Divine Duvet.* Invest in a pretty new duvet or bedspread. It will freshen up the room instantly.
- *Pillow Pizzazz.* Some new pillows and pillowcases that coordinate with your sheets and duvet will add softness to your bed.
- *Flower Finesse.* Buy some fresh flowers and put them in a favorite vase.
- *Candle Cozy.* A few flickering candles will add instant romance to your new B&B bedroom.

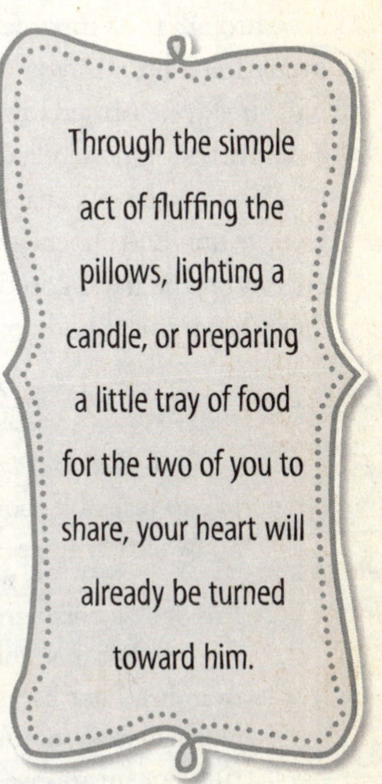
Through the simple act of fluffing the pillows, lighting a candle, or preparing a little tray of food for the two of you to share, your heart will already be turned toward him.

- *Music Magic.* Now for some light jazz or classical music to set the tone for the evening.
- *TV Tune-out.* Unless you and your mate purposely choose to watch a funny or romantic movie together, turn the TV off.
- *Tray of Delights.* Bring in a drink and cheese tray with some fresh fruit, dim the lights, and you're on your way to a lovely and romantic stay in your very own Bed-and-Breakfast Inn bedroom. Enjoy!

It Really Is the Little Things

Whatever little touches you decide to incorporate into your homemade B&B, this is one project where you don't have to worry about your husband's reaction. This is more about adjusting your attitude and enhancing your space than getting a *wow* from your guy.

Through the simple act of fluffing the pillows, lighting a candle, or preparing a little tray of food for the two of you to share, your heart will already be turned toward him. Everybody benefits from a relaxing environment (and a relaxed wife).

Why not have a snack to share when he gets home? Some of his favorite nuts and chocolates up in your room or some cheese and crackers out on the patio could be just the transition he needs after a long day. Or try this if perhaps he'd enjoy something a little sweeter:

Chocolate Dipped Fruit

1 11½-ounce package (2 cups) milk chocolate morsels
¼ cup vegetable shortening
Strawberries, grapes, bananas, apples, kiwi, or pineapple

In a double boiler, melt milk chocolate morsels and shortening over hot (not boiling) water; stir until smooth. Remove from heat, but keep over hot water. (If chocolate thickens, return to heat; stir until smooth.) Makes 1 cup melted chocolate. For microwave method, melt on high 1 minute; stir. Repeat.

Dip pieces of fruit into chocolate; gently shake off excess. Place on foil-lined cookie sheets. Chill 10-15 minutes until chocolate is set. Peel off foil. Fruit may be kept at room temperature up to 1 hour. If chocolate coating becomes sticky, return fruit to refrigerator.

Prayer for Today

Dear God, remind me to treat my husband with more care and honor than any guest who comes into our home.

Getting Creative

- My husband loves a special kind of root beer that we cannot keep stocked in the house. (With four teenagers it's hard to keep them from eating or drinking anything within their line of sight.) If I want to make sure he can have a cold drink after work, I hide his root beer under the veggies in the crisper—no chance of the kids looking there.
- If your husband gets home before you do, plan ahead by hiding a treat in the fridge for him. Call during the day to let him know that it's waiting for him.

Project Reports

"This past Friday I set out all of my husband's favorite snacks so when he arrived home he was greeted with food and beverage. I had to pick up one of our children so was not home right when he got home. When I arrived home I was greeted at the door with a very nice kiss. I know he appreciates the thought that goes into making his homecoming special."—Sue

Your Plan for the Project *(copy your plan on The Husband Project Planner at the back of this book)*

Your Results *(his reaction, my reaction, etc.)*

Project 20

Post-it Notes, Man's Greatest Invention

Leave a Word of Encouragement

"A simple word can renew hope."
LOIS MAYDAY RABEY

Your Project

Leave a cute and flirty note for your husband to find.

Keep it simple today. Put a Post-it in his briefcase, on his dashboard, in his wallet, anywhere that he will find it. Make it fun, make it flirty, but just make sure *he* is the one who will find it. Wink-wink.

OK—some guys are going to think it's hokey. But if you can't be hokey in your marriage, when can you be?

All I want you to do is give him a little encouragement. I know there's nothing more encouraging for my husband than knowing that I'm on his side. Throughout his day, I want him to know that no matter how difficult things may be at work, he's got someone at home rooting for him. All it takes is a Post-it note and about two seconds of thought.

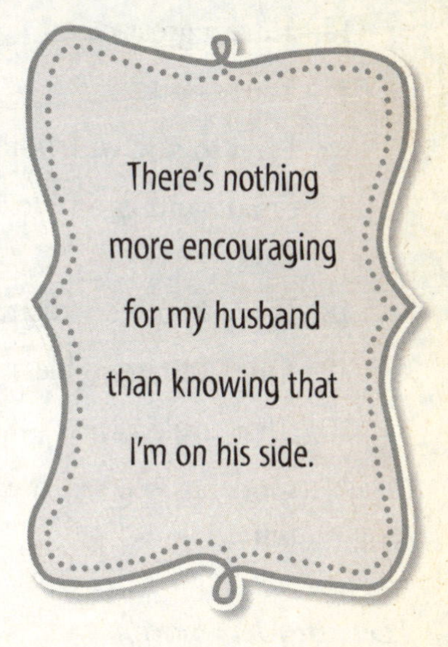

Crib Notes: 21 Post-it-Sized Encouragements

1. I'm praying for you today.

2. Those jeans are really working for you...
3. I love you.
4. You are the best dad!
5. You're the kind of husband that makes the other wives jealous.
6. You rock my world!
7. Can't wait to see you tonight—meet me upstairs...
8. Thanks for working hard to provide for us. I appreciate all that you do.
9. You make me feel beautiful.
10. I thank God for you every day.
11. How did I get so lucky, being married to a guy like you?
12. You're great!
13. You make every day more fun.
14. Have a great day.
15. You're hot!
16. I feel so safe with you.
17. Smart and good looking—I've got the whole package in you!
18. You can be very distracting, you know...
19. Our kids are so blessed to have a dad like you.
20. That smile I wear—it's all because of you.
21. God has blessed me in big ways by letting me be your wife.

Let's Be More Specific

I gave you that list in case this whole exercise is a challenge for you. If it feels uncomfortable leaving a note for your husband, if you get writer's block even when the blank page is Post-it note sized, just use one of the above phrases to get you started.

However, if you're comfortable and can get a little more personal, I highly encourage you to do so.

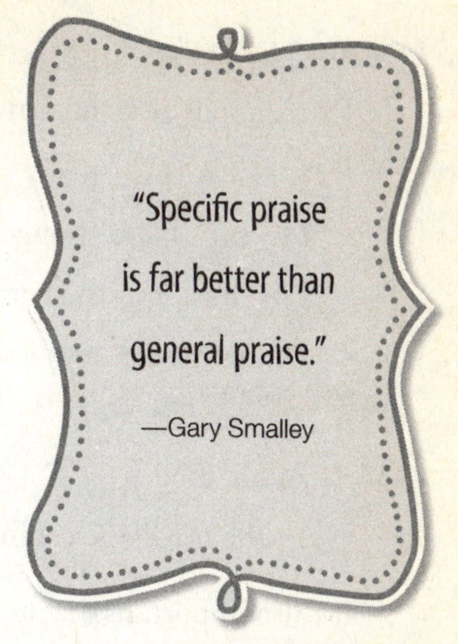

I keep a stash of cards underneath my bed. If I want to let my guy know something specific that has encouraged me, and I don't think a Post-it is big enough to hold it all, I pull out one of the cards to give myself room to let him know how much I love him.

When leaving notes for my husband, I try to be as specific as possible about how he has blessed me. Every once in a while, I will leave him a little note saying things like,

> "How lucky am I that I have a husband who makes the bed every day. Thanks for taking care of me." (Hint: Men love to know that you feel "taken care of." It makes guys feel like they're doing their job.)
>
> Or
>
> "I loved falling asleep on your shoulder last night. You have a special way of making me feel safe and warm."

Think about the ways that your husband loves you, and then put them down on paper. When you write those things down, it's a double blessing because while you're writing them down, they remind you of how much you are loved, and they encourage your husband in a way that only you can.

Prayer for Today

Wherever he is, God, remind my husband that he is loved and thought of.

Getting Creative

Think about your husband's day and all the places he might find the note:

- His car's spare change tray
- His drawer in the bathroom
- Under his car keys
- Your mailbox
- In his shoe
- In the medicine cabinet

It's also important that he find it when no one else is around. I once decorated my husband's lunch bag with hearts and little notes saying how much I loved him. He took the opportunity to let me know that it was better if we kept those things private.

You know your husband and how he reacts to PDAs (Public Displays of Affection). Make sure that anything you do makes him burn only with love—never with embarrassment.

Project Reports

> "I had planned to put a note in his suitcase for his trip to LA, but I didn't have time to pull it together. (We are so loaded with responsibilities with our three teenagers and one preteen that we can't seem to get the daily stuff done.) So instead, I will decorate his home office with romantic notes. This project also got me thinking about the many sweet and incredibly romantic things he did for me when we were dating and newly married. I know that it will stir up memories for him too."—Elaine

Your Plan for the Project *(copy your plan on The Husband Project Planner at the back of this book)*

Your Results *(his reaction, my reaction, etc.)*

Project 21

Car Chases and Karate Chops

It's Guy Movie Night

Kathleen Kelly (Meg Ryan): *"What is it with men and* The Godfather?"

Joe Fox (Tom Hanks): "The Godfather *is the I Ching.* The Godfather *is the sum of all wisdom.* The Godfather *is the answer to any question. What should I pack for my summer vacation? 'Leave the gun, take the cannoli.'"*

You've Got Mail

Your Project

Let him win the media wars as you suggest an action-packed-car-chasing-things-exploding thriller.

One of the most marriage-testing conversations a couple can have takes place in the aisles of your local video store. You want romance and subtitles; he wants guns and grunts. In no area of marriage is it harder to "die to self" than when picking what you'll be watching on a Friday night.

The good news? Choosing to watch a "guy flick" with your man reaps double benefits—not only are you loving on your husband in a tangible way, you're also doing research at the same time. The more Rambo-esque cinema you take in, the deeper a peek you'll have into your man's inner life.

If you ever doubted that your husband's deepest desire was to be your hero, just check out the kinds of movies he watches. Most male-movie fare is all about being a stand-up kind of guy, doing the right

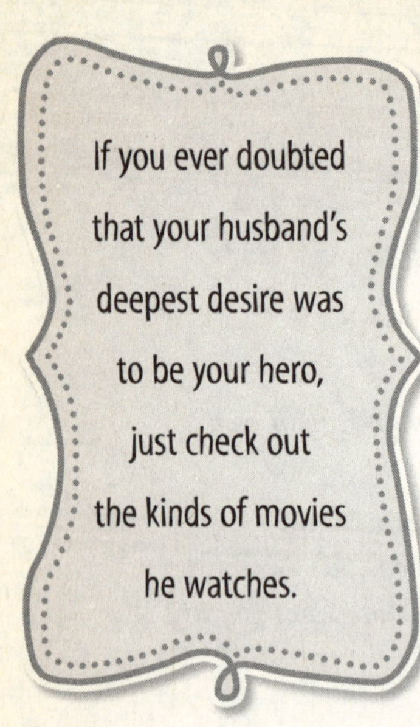

thing, no matter the circumstances. (Think Bruce Willis in *Die Hard* and Mel Gibson in *The Patriot.*)

So in the interest of public service to the wife community, I've compiled a list of the best dude movies as voted on by my guy friends. You may not like, or even approve of, every title on this list, but at least you'll have a working knowledge of guy movie culture, plus a go-to guide the next time he leaves it up to you to fend for yourself at the video store.

Thanks to my guy friends for their insight and comments. They have performed a great service to women everywhere.

Guy Movies

- Anything with Al Pacino
- Anything with Marlon Brando (pre-*Don Juan Demarco*)
- Anything with Bruce Willis

Sports

- *Field of Dreams* ("Baseball. Need I say more?"—Steve)
- *We Are Marshall* ("Inspiring, true sports story."—Scott)

Action

- *Back to the Future* trilogy ("I've always been interested in time travel. The only thing that would have made it better would be a cameo by Molly Ringwald."—Steve)
- *Mission Impossible 1,2,3*
- *Bourne Supremacy* and all the sequels
- *The Net*

Violence

- *Gladiator* ("Total macho movie, lots of action. However, good plot, and I love the soundtrack. This is one of the few movies where you don't mind being the guy wearing the skirt."—Karl)

- *Saving Private Ryan* ("Groundbreaking cinema, pro-military without being pro-war."—Steve)

- *The Shawshank Redemption* ("Morgan Freeman and good over evil. What more could you ask for?"—Charles)

  (Note from Kathi: While these movies are the hardest for me to watch, they do give me ample opportunity to bury my face in my husband's shoulder.)

Humor

- *Young Frankenstein* ("Seriously funny movie. Quotes are memorable and make me laugh out loud whenever I think about that movie."—Karl)
- *Ocean's 11*

Romance

This is a trick category. If you think this falls under guy movies, you're still thinking like a chick.

Movies Both Guys and Girls Like

This is a magical list. Every Hollywood producer is looking for that mystical intersection of entertaining males and delighting females. Here's a group of movies that, from my research, is a pretty sure bet for both of you:

- *Princess Bride* (Don't let the title fool you. Even the teenage boys in our home love this movie.)

- *What's Up, Doc?*
- *Indiana Jones* (1, 3, and 4, but don't even bother with 2)
- *City Slickers*
- *Field of Dreams*
- *Shrek*

Chick Flicks

To be watched only with girlfriends and large supplies of tissues and chocolates:

- *An Affair to Remember*
- *Breakfast at Tiffany's*
- *Steel Magnolias*
- *Fried Green Tomatoes*
- *Say Anything* (John Cusack declaring his eternal love with a boom box? It's the fantasy of many a girl and the impossible-to-live-up-to standard for every guy.)
- Anything with Meg Ryan
- Anything written by Jane Austen

Prayer for Today

Dear God, help me enjoy the things that my husband enjoys. Let him see that I try to connect with him in ways that are big and small.

Getting Creative

- It doesn't matter if this happens at home or at the local Cineplex. Just find the movie and go.
- Don't want your husband's suspicions to be aroused? Perhaps get two movies—one that you both agree on and one just for him.

Project Reports

"Both my husband and I sit through mostly G-rated movies every Friday evening, as we share Family Movie Night with our young boys. And because my husband flies on business frequently, he has plenty of chances to watch his guy movies. Can you see where this is going? I'm the one who rarely gets to watch "my" movies...but I will make my best effort to sit through a sports film with my husband. I just don't think I can take another Bruce Willis or Steven Seagal film. I'll have to pray about this...a lot."—Teresa

"My husband is into martial arts, so I said, 'Hey, let's watch one of your fight movies' (I don't know what else to call them). So he said, 'OK.' I thought I would truly hate it, but I found out it was fun to snuggle in bed and have him explain the movie to me. We both loved it. Felt like I was on a date!"—Strawberry

"This one had an incredible outcome. At our house, with three teenagers and one preteen, I usually wash dishes, fold laundry, or bake muffins while my husband is relaxing by watching a movie. He always invites me to join him on the couch to watch, but I always say, 'I have too much to do.' So by the time the movie is over, he is relaxed and ready for romance, and I am exhausted and ready for sleep.

"Well, I tried the 'movie night' idea. I let him pick out a movie, and I left the dishes and the laundry and sat next to him for the whole movie. Guess what? By the time the movie was over, I was ready for romance! We had the most romantic evening that we've had in a long time. This little activity showed me that I can't expect to feel romantic if I don't take some time to relax. I already rented a movie for tonight."—Elaine

Your Plan for the Project *(copy your plan on The Husband Project Planner at the back of this book)*

Your Results *(his reaction, my reaction, etc.)*

Bonus Project 3

Sex

I Think We're Alone Now

"I don't mind what people do as long as they don't do it in the street and frighten the horses."
JENNIE JEROME CHURCHILL (MOTHER OF WINSTON CHURCHILL)

Your Bonus Project

Figure out some time this week for initiating sex with your guy when the two of you are alone.

Time to clear out the house. If you have kids, send them to Grandma's house for the night or swap babysitting for the evening with another worn-out mom. Your kiddos get a sleepover—and so do you.

I would love to say it gets easier as the kids get older, but with three teenagers in our house, we seem to be "kids free" about as often as our sons decide that it would be a great day to clean their room. While they're all busy with their own lives, it is a rare moment when one of them isn't sleeping, eating, reading, studying, or watching TV somewhere in the house.

Which is not conducive to romance.

We have employed every method of soundproofing that we can think of. We turn the TV up full volume and put ourselves on low volume. We sneak and *shush!* and do what we have to do—the whole time knowing that at any moment there could be a knock on the door with the question, "Can I get a ride to the mall?"

Romance is so much more fun when the real possibility of being interrupted has been removed. An occasional rendezvous at a local hotel fits the bill nicely.

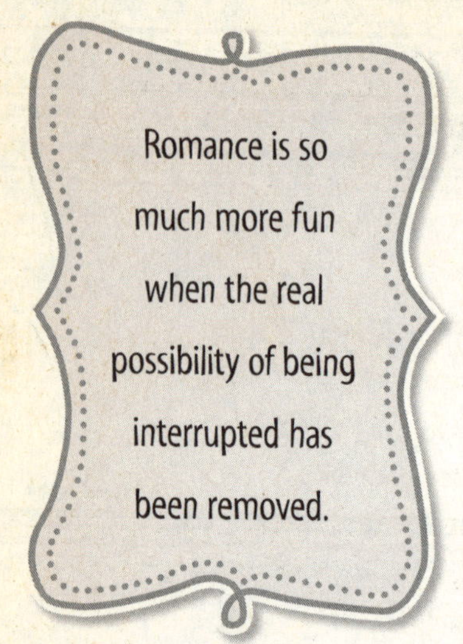

If you have a regular Bunko game, skip it. Cancel appointments with your friends and make one with your husband. Let him know early in the day what you're planning for tonight. This could be one of his better workdays in a long time.

Put your cell phones on silent and shut down the computers. Make romance the priority however it has to happen.

Prayer for Today

Dear God, help me to make my sexual relationship with my husband a priority not just in my heart and mind, but also in my schedule.

Getting Creative

- If an evening is going to be too hard to swing, how about both of you coming home for lunch. Send him back to work with a smile on his face.
- Does your husband work too far from home to make the round trip? How about being super-extravagant and make a dream of his come true. Plan on meeting him for lunch near his office, and at the last minute call him with a location change. Find a hotel close to his office where you can really be alone.
- Maybe all you need is a morning with no agenda. If it's a sleep-in Saturday or a morning where neither of you has to be anywhere, skip your morning at the gym and get a workout at home.

Project Reports

"A babysitter who can take the kids overnight is worth her weight in gold! We hire an overnight babysitter probably twice a year (the kids spend the night at her house, not ours) so we can have free run of the house. Not only do we get free run of the house, sleeping in is a great bonus after a late night of activity."—Marie

"Once or twice a month my husband goes into work late so that we can have the house to ourselves for a couple of hours. Enough said."—Katie

"*So* I initiated sex last week and my husband was pleased. Since he works on our remodel most evenings, he showers before bed and this time he didn't shower alone. The funny thing is that he thought that was the surprise. I had to scold him right back to the bedroom and out of his jammies!"—Stacie

Your Plan for the Project *(copy your plan on The Husband Project Planner at the back of this book)*

Your Results *(his reaction, my reaction, etc.)*

Wrap Up

Congratulations! You have gone where not many women have gone before—21 days of loving your husband on purpose. I am sure by now you've seen many of the benefits that other wives have seen by working the projects:

- A new habit of thinking about how you can bless your husband, every day.
- The realization that sometimes it takes only a moment to bless your husband on a busy day.
- The realization of how you already were blessing your husband.
- A reminder of some of the reasons that you fell in love with your husband in the first place.
- A much better lingerie wardrobe.

I don't want this to be the end for you. My prayer is that blessing your husband has become a habit that you have every intention of keeping. But just like our intentions of eating more vegetables and exercising every day, it's so much easier to slip back into old routines.

Here are a few ideas to keep you focused on your husband long after The Husband Project is over:

- **Keep up the accountability**. Ask your accountability partners if they want to continue to check in once a week to make sure you keep on blessing your husband.

- **Put reminders on your calendar.** Chocolates in bed on Thursday? Lingerie every Saturday? Scatter a few reminders throughout your month so that your husband is constantly reminded of how much he is on your mind.
- **Establish an All-About-Him Day once a week.** Wednesdays are all about Roger. I try to make sure that I'm cooking something for dinner that I know my husband will love (this usually involves some large hunk of meat that looks like it came straight out of a *Flintstones* cartoon). I also make sure to give him a call on Wednesdays to let him know I'm thinking about him.
- **Commit to doing The Husband Project once a year.** Make sure you get your money's worth out of this book. Use it over and over again to refocus yourself once a year on your husband's needs.

Tools of The Husband Project

The Husband Project Planner

Consider this the place to put the Cliff Notes of your Husband Project. Project managers have told me over and over that it was great to have their entire plan laid out on just a couple of pieces of paper so they could make copies and refer to it often.

- Write down one or two sentences about what your plan is for each day.
- Make copies of this plan to share with your accountability partners to help keep you on track.
- Make some extra copies for yourself. Leave one at the office, one in your purse, and one in your Bible. That way, no matter where you are, you'll know what your project is for today and be able to plan for what is coming up.
- As you complete the projects, make sure you give yourself a checkmark on your planner. Nothing feels quite as satisfying on a busy day as a "project accomplished" checkmark.

Week One

Sunday: Project 1 ☐ check when completed
Your plan for the project:

Monday: Project 2 ☐ check when completed
Your plan for the project:

Tuesday: Project 3 ☐ check when completed
Your plan for the project:

Wednesday: Project 4 ☐ check when completed
Your plan for the project:

Thursday: Project 5 ☐ check when completed
Your plan for the project:

Friday: Project 6 ☐ check when completed
Your plan for the project:

Saturday: Project 7 ☐ check when completed
Your plan for the project:

Bonus Project 1 ☐ check when completed
Your plan for the project:

Week Two

Sunday: Project 8 ☐ check when completed
Your plan for the project:

Monday: Project 9 ☐ check when completed
Your plan for the project:

Tuesday: Project 10 ☐ check when completed
Your plan for the project:

Wednesday: Project 11 ☐ check when completed
Your plan for the project:

Thursday: Project 12 ☐ check when completed
Your plan for the project:

Friday: Project 13 ☐ check when completed
Your plan for the project:

Saturday: Project 14 ☐ check when completed
Your plan for the project:

Bonus Project 2 ☐ check when completed
Your plan for the project:

Week Three

Sunday: Project 15 ☐ check when completed

Your plan for the project:

Monday: Project 16 ☐ check when completed

Your plan for the project:

Tuesday: Project 17 ☐ check when completed

Your plan for the project:

Wednesday: Project 18 ☐ check when completed

Your plan for the project:

Thursday: Project 19 ☐ check when completed

Your plan for the project:

Friday: Project 20 ☐ check when completed

Your plan for the project:

Saturday: Project 21 ☐ check when completed

Your plan for the project:

Bonus Project 3 ☐ check when completed

Your plan for the project:

The Real Woman's Guide to Lingerie Shopping

Jill Swanson, author of Simply Beautiful: Inside and Out

WWW.JILLSWANSON.COM

While lingerie is often considered a matter of personal preference, there are some ways to accentuate the positive, and at the very least, *minimize* the negative—taking you from stagnant to stunning in the bedroom.

First of all, focus on what you believe to be the best feature of your body. Is it the shape of your legs? Your curvy shoulders? Symmetrical breasts? Smooth skin? Feminine feet? Sexy ankles? Rich hair color? Sculpted facial features? Cute belly button? Voluptuous proportions? Or perhaps it's the unique asymmetrical piece of art that you are? We all have something (or several things) that stand out as our best feature.

Second, learn to love it. When it comes to lingerie in the bedroom, it's legal to exploit it. Here are a few tips to enhance what you have:

1. *Line and Design:* Nighties with wide shoulder straps that extend to the outer edges of your shoulders, or teeter on the perimeter of your shoulders giving a V effect, can make lower areas appear smaller as the eye moves down toward the waist and hips.
2. *Waist-not, Want-not:* If you have a fuller waist, use something fun and cute like a shorter "baby doll" type top that floats over that area, but drops the eyes to those curvy

hips and great legs. A definable waist should be shown off with pieces that nip in on the sides and emphasize your shapeliness.

3. *Balancing the Backside:* Make sure that a round derriere is flattered by styles that gently hug the area rather than camouflage it. A flat derriere can be balanced with a playful, short flouncy skirt or ruffled panties.

4. *Rosebuds and Blossoms:* Small chests are flattered most with padding under the bust and a lacy overlay—it's a great way to make mountains out of molehills. A full chest may need to be wrangled a bit with something uplifting that pulls your breasts together. Look for a bra within the garment that has support on the sides and bottom. Remember—"bolster your holster" for a dramatic effect!

5. *The Long and Short of It.* If you are tall, revel in it and break up your look with horizontal jewelry. Bejewel the waist with a chain belt, the ankles with bracelets, and add necklaces and upper arm bracelets (be a 21st-century Cleopatra!). If you're not so tall or have short legs, go for the long and sleek look with a longer nightgown that skims the body and has a high slit; finish the look with a pair of stiletto heel slippers.

6. *Feminine Mystique:* Always leave something to the imagination! If your man can see everything in the treasure chest, where's the incentive to go on the hunt? Strategically placed lace, bows, or sheer overlays of chiffon are wonderful ways to feed his curiosity.

7. *Make it Fun:* Give him a little something to undo, whether it's a lace-up bodice, a garter belt, or long hair pinned on top of your head.

8. *Be Creative:* Sometimes the most sexy lingerie you can wear is an everyday shirt or dress with nothing underneath, or

a body shaper that gives you shape by day and attitude by night.

9. *Surprise Him:* If you're assertive and wear a lot of dark colors, pull out a demure pink camisole. If you're quiet and conservative, try a bold color like red or an animal print and let your wild side come to the surface. Play dress up. This is the one place you can let your imagination run wild!

As women we have to learn to love our bodies the way they are—no matter what condition they're in. Cellulite, scars, extra padding, or loose muscle tone, remember that a man doesn't see what we focus on when it comes to our bodies and bedroom attire.

I have an abdomen that looks like a road map of New York City. Nine surgeries have taken their toll, but I've learned to accept it for the most part and creatively camouflage it when it does bother me.

Above all, choose styles and colors that make you feel glamorous, romantic, and confident.

A Chick's Guide to Guy Food

Here are some of our favorite recipes that are sure to be guy pleasers.

The Real, the Original, the Authentic...
Chocolate Chip Cookie Recipe

2¼ cups all-purpose flour
1 teaspoon baking soda
1 teaspoon salt
1 cup butter, softened (2 sticks, ½ pound)
¾ cup granulated white sugar
¾ cup packed brown sugar
1 teaspoon vanilla extract
2 eggs
2 cups semisweet chocolate morsels (12-ounce package)
1 cup chopped nuts

COMBINE flour, baking soda, and salt in small bowl. Beat butter, granulated sugar, brown sugar, and vanilla in large mixer bowl. Add eggs one at a time, beating well after each addition; gradually beat in flour mixture. Stir in morsels and nuts. Drop by rounded tablespoon onto ungreased baking sheets.

BAKE in preheated 375° F oven for 9 to 11 minutes or until golden brown. Let stand for 2 minutes; remove to wire racks to cool completely.

PAN COOKIE VARIATION: PREPARE dough as above. Spread into greased 10x15 jelly-roll pan. Bake in preheated 375° F oven for 20 to 25 minutes or until golden brown. Cool in pan on wire rack.

FOR HIGH ALTITUDE BAKING (>5,200 feet): INCREASE flour to 2½ cups; add 2 teaspoonfuls water with flour; reduce both granulated sugar and brown sugar to ⅔ cup each. Bake at 375° F, drop cookies for 8 to 10 minutes and pan cookies for 17 to 19 minutes.

Thank you to project manager Karmyn for this delicious recipe:

Deluxe Chicken Breasts

Nothing fancy, just tender chicken breasts drizzled with a delicious cheese sauce that are good enough to add to your list of weekly specials.

Preparation time: 30 minutes
Cook time: 15 minutes

Serves 4

Main ingredients:
½ cup all-purpose flour
¼ cup dry bread crumbs
2 egg whites, lightly beaten
2 tablespoons water
4 boneless, skinless chicken breasts (approximately 4 ounces each)
2 tablespoons vegetable oil

For the sauce:
2 tablespoons butter
1 tablespoon all-purpose flour
1 cup skim milk
½ cup shredded cheddar cheese

Preheat oven to 350° F. Combine flour and bread crumbs in a shallow flat dish. In a shallow bowl, whisk together egg whites and water. Dip chicken in egg white/water mixture, then dredge in bread crumb mixture, coating all sides. In large skillet, heat oil over medium-high heat. Add chicken; cook, turning once, until browned (about 5 minutes on each side). Place chicken in a lightly greased shallow baking dish. Bake at 350° F until cooked through, approximately 15 minutes.

To prepare sauce, melt butter in a small saucepan over medium heat. Stir in flour until well combined. Slowly add milk, stirring constantly until thickened (about 8 to 10 minutes). Remove from heat; stir in cheddar cheese. (The heat of the sauce will melt cheese.)

Place chicken breasts on serving tray. Drizzle with sauce. Serve immediately. Mmmmm!

Cheddar Dip with Smoked Sausages

2 tablespoons unsalted butter
½ cup finely chopped sweet onion
½ cup smoked sausage, cut into ½-inch pieces
2 tablespoons Dijon or whole-grain mustard
8-ounce package cream cheese
4 cups shredded sharp white cheddar cheese
6 drops hot pepper sauce

Lightly coat a 1-quart baking dish with cooking spray.

In a medium saucepan over medium-high heat, melt the butter. Add the onion and sauté for 2 minutes or until the onion begins to soften. Add the sausage and cook until cooked through, about 8 to 10 minutes. Drain away and discard any fat.

Add the mustard and cream cheese, then stir until melted. Remove the pan from the heat and stir in the cheddar cheese, a handful at a time, until blended

Stir in the hot sauce, then transfer to the prepared baking dish. Let cool, then cover and refrigerate for up to 3 days.

When ready to serve, preheat oven to 350° F. While the oven heats, let the dip sit at room temperature for about 30 minutes. Bake the dip for 20 to 25 minutes, or until bubbling. Serve warm. Servings: 6 to 8.

Farmer's Breakfast Casserole

2½ cups frozen shredded hash brown potatoes or Tater Tots
¾ cup shredded Monterey Jack with (optional) jalapeño peppers
1 package Knorr Leek recipe mix
1 cup chopped fully cooked ham or Canadian bacon (optional)
¼ cup sliced green onion
4 eggs beaten or 1 cup egg substitute
1 12-ounce can evaporated milk (or 1½ cups evaporated skim milk)
¼ teaspoon pepper
⅛ teaspoon salt (or seasoning substitute)
½ pound asparagus or mushrooms, washed and cut into 1-inch pieces
4 to 5 tomatoes, coarsely chopped

Spray a 2-quart square baking dish with PAM or other cooking spray. Arrange potatoes evenly in the bottom of the dish. Sprinkle cheese, ham, and green onion over all. In a mixing bowl combine eggs, evaporated milk, pepper, salt, and Knorr Leek mix. Pour over mixture in baking dish. Sprinkle with Jane's Krazy Mixed-Up Salt or Mrs. Dash Original Blend. Cover with foil or plastic wrap and refrigerate overnight. Next morning bake uncovered at 350° F for 30 minutes. Remove from oven; add asparagus or mushrooms and tomatoes. Bake for another 30 minutes until golden brown. Let stand 5 minutes before serving.

Slow Cooker Stew

1½ pounds stew meat
1 large onion, chopped
3 carrots, chopped
2 stalks celery, chopped
4 medium potatoes, peeled and cut into cubes
1 can (28 ounces) whole tomatoes (undrained)
1 tablespoon Worcestershire sauce
2 tablespoons parsley flakes
1 teaspoon salt
½ teaspoon pepper
3 cloves garlic, finely chopped (optional)
2 tablespoons quick cooking tapioca

Brown stew meat in a pot on top of the stove, seasoning to choice with salt, pepper, and garlic (optional). Transfer meat to the slow cooker. Add remaining ingredients, stirring to blend. Cover and cook on low for 8 hours until meat is tender.

Quaker Oats Prize-Winning Meatloaf

1½ pounds ground beef
¾ cup oats, uncooked
¼ cup onion, chopped
1½ teaspoon salt
¼ teaspoon pepper
1 cup tomato juice
1 egg, beaten

Combine all ingredients and pack firmly into an ungreased loaf pan. Bake in a preheated 350° F oven for 1 hour and 15 minutes. Let stand 5 minutes before slicing. Serves 4.

Dear Reader,

Thanks for being a part of *The Husband Project.* It is my prayer that between this book and your efforts, God will bless your marriage in ways you never would expect.

I would love to hear more about how you have used *The Husband Project.* Here are some ways that we can stay in contact:

- For speaking invitations, contact our office at speaking@kathilipp.com, check out my website at www.kathilipp.com, or call 408-960-7415. Or write me at:

  Kathi Lipp
  171 Branham Lane
  Suite 10-122,
  San Jose, CA 95136

- Opportunities for input and discussion with other readers are available at www.thehusbandproject.org.
- If you are leading a group in *The Husband Project,* check out the "For Leaders" section at www.thehusbandproject.org.
- Finally, you can reach me directly at kathi@kathilipp.com.

In His Grace,

Kathi Lipp